MAKING IT WORK

The keys to success for young people living independently

Jamie Harding

This book is dedicated to my grandmother, Elizabeth May Harding

First published in Great Britain in June 2004 by

The Policy Press
University of Bristol
Fourth Floor
Beacon House
Queen's Road
Bristol BS8 1QU
UK

Tel +44 (0)117 331 4054
Fax +44 (0)117 331 4093
e-mail tpp-info@bristol.ac.uk
www.policypress.org.uk

British Library Cataloguing in Publication Data
A catalogue record for this book is available from the British Library.

Library of Congress Cataloging-in-Publication Data
A catalog record for this book has been requested.

ISBN 1 86134 532 1 paperback

Jamie Harding is a Senior Lecturer in Housing at the School of the Built Environment, Northumbria University, UK.

Cover design by Qube Design Associates, Bristol.
Front cover: photograph supplied by kind permission of www.third-avenue.co.uk
Printed and bound in Great Britain by Hobbs the Printers Ltd, Southampton.

Contents

List of tables and figures

Tables

Figures

Acknowledgements

I would like to thank the following people for their assistance in the writing of this book:

The academic staff who have provided valuable advice and assistance, particularly Dr Robert Hollands, Professor Michael Hill, John Kennedy, Dr Robert MacDonald, Dr Peter Selman, Dr Rachel Kirk, Andrea Willett and Rahat Ambreen.

All the staff of the local authority who have given up time to assist with the project, particularly Michael Ball, Neil Munslow, Paul Keenan, Ann Atkinson, David Robertson and Simon Colligan.

The interviewers who showed so much commitment: Ruth Diggle, Alan Wallace, Liz Richley, Judith Miller and especially Joe Sharkey.

Nicola Sugden, Carla Franchie and Jacqui Sirs of the Newcastle Independence Network, together with staff from First Move and the Support Needs Assessment Project, who provided much useful information.

Kim McMasters and other staff of In Line for the thorough reports that they provided on their services.

The SPAT workers for the substantial information that they recorded.

The staff of Cumberland House for responding so quickly to requests for information.

Karen Bowler and Dawn Rushen of The Policy Press for their advice and encouragement.

Allison for her constant support and Christopher and Kelly for coping with my attention being elsewhere.

The young people themselves for being prepared to give up their time to discuss their circumstances.

ONE

Young people in independent tenancies: an issue that must be faced

In the summer of 2002, local authorities were given new responsibilities to secure housing for homeless 16- and 17-year-olds. Under the 1985 Housing Act, a duty to secure accommodation (a duty that was weakened then restored by subsequent legislation) had been owed to applicants who satisfied four conditions. These conditions were that the applicant was homeless, had not become homeless intentionally, had a local connection with the authority that they had approached and was in priority need. The Act and the accompanying Code of Guidance indicated that an applicant was considered to be in priority need if their household included dependent children, a person who was pregnant or someone who was vulnerable for some other reason (Pleace et al, 1997, p 3).

Historically, there was no clear indication as to which young people should be considered vulnerable, and so be regarded as being in priority need (Pleace and Quilgars, 1999, p 97). However, in April 2000, the government changed the Code of Guidance to indicate that the Secretary of State expected most 16- and 17-year-olds to be regarded as "vulnerable" (DTLR, 2000). While local authorities are only required to "have regard" to the Code of Guidance, this change of approach became a legal obligation in the summer of 2002 as a result of the 2002 Homelessness (Priority Need for Accommodation) (England) Order, which placed all 16- and 17-year-olds in the priority need category (Statutory Instrument 2002 No 2051)[1].

Treating all 16- and 17-year-olds as being in priority need was a step that some authorities had taken voluntarily: Venn (1985, pp 18-20) noted that five authorities – including Newcastle – extended the priority need categories on the grounds of age. By the time of a further study by Kay (1994, p 2), 23% of authorities were accepting that homeless 16- and 17-year-olds were vulnerable because of their age alone. However, the implementation of the 2002 statutory instrument means that the majority of housing authorities are faced with securing more accommodation for 16- and 17-year-olds.

There is evidence to suggest that authorities will need to find extra accommodation for this age group themselves, rather than discharging their duties by making referrals to other landlords. Bevan et al (1995) found that many private landlords did not want to let to young, single people. Since their study, restrictions to Housing Benefit entitlement for the under 25s reduced further the number of private landlords making lettings to this age group (Chugg, 1998, p 5; DETR, 1999a). The Housing Corporation (1996) found that nearly two thirds of housing associations had made some lettings or placements to homeless 16- and 17-year-olds and care leavers, and some associations had stock set aside for this age group. However, Third et al (2001, p 98) showed that young people were underrepresented as housing association tenants in the South Clyde area. In addition, the relatively small size of the housing association sector suggests that local authorities will be forced to make the majority of lettings to 16- and 17-year-olds from their own stock.

The areas that cannot follow this pattern are those where there has been a total transfer of the ownership or management of local authority housing. By the summer of 2002, there had been 156 large-scale voluntary transfers (LSVTs) of local authority stock to housing associations (ODPM, 2002). The present government has encouraged the creation of Arm's Length Management Organisations (ALMOs), which take on the day-to-day management of the local authority stock, although the authority retains ownership. In 2003, the government gave approval for 13 authorities – including Newcastle upon Tyne – to create ALMOs, subject to satisfactory inspection ratings (ODPM, 2003a). In areas where the ownership or management of all the local authority housing has been transferred, there is a contractual agreement for the housing association or ALMO to provide housing for homeless households[2].

This study is important as it is the first to provide a quantitative evaluation of the factors that can make the difference between success and failure in independent tenancies among 16- and 17-year-olds[3]. Although it is acknowledged that failure is likely to have a severely detrimental effect on individuals, the evaluation is made mainly from the perspective of the landlord. The failure of young people's tenancies is particularly disadvantageous at a time when many local authorities are struggling to fill empty properties. A series of recent studies (for example, Keenan et al, 1999; Power and Mumford, 1999) have highlighted the tendency towards the abandonment of rented property in inner-city areas of the North of England. These difficulties have been aggravated by an increasingly rapid turnover of council tenancies, which results in financial losses arising from properties standing empty, together with security and repair costs (Pawson, 1998).

In this study, unsuccessful outcomes of tenancies are defined as those that impose increased costs on the landlord, that is, rapid turnover of tenancies, abandonment of properties, evictions and repeat homelessness. The need to improve tenancy outcomes among 16- and 17-year-olds is particularly urgent because, as Third et al (2001, p 47) note:

> The risk of 'tenancy failure' among young single people is clearly well above average, though for young single parents the figures are less clear cut. As might be expected, propensity to sustain tenancies is also particularly low for the 16-19 age group.

Similarly, in Cairns's (2001) study, local authority staff believed that young single people being unable to maintain tenancies was a factor leading to repeated applications as homeless. Indeed, it is in the context of homelessness that discussions of success and failure in independent tenancies most frequently take place – as will be seen in the next chapter, many of the government's views about independent living emerge from policy documents concerned with preventing homelessness and resettling homeless people.

There has been little coordination of the response to the perceived difficulties in independent tenancies – Quilgars and Pleace (1999, pp 112-13) argue that housing and support services for young people have tended to develop in a responsive, ad hoc manner at a local level. There also seems to be little consensus as to the needs that services are intended to meet. An examination of the limited literature on the subject suggests that difficulties in young people's tenancies have been attributed to three types of factor: failings on the part of the individual, structural failings and failings in informal support.

Failings on the part of the individual

Harding (1999, p 68) quotes one local authority officer who implied that support for young people in independent housing is necessary to protect the landlord from the consequences of antisocial behaviour:

> You need supported housing to protect your investment, otherwise you find your property being trashed.

However, it is more common in discussions of young people's experience of living independently to suggest that it is their inexperience or immaturity – rather than any deviant tendencies – that is likely to result in difficulties, which may in turn lead to homelessness. For example, Biehal and Wade (1999, p 87) argue that a reason for homelessness among their sample of care leavers was that "many were ill-prepared or unready for independent living".

The provision of support is frequently advocated as a means of overcoming the perceived inexperience of young people. Hutson (1999, p 216) suggests that homeless 16- and 17-year-olds are felt to need support because of their age alone. In Harding's (1999) study, eight of 19 local authority officers responsible for dealing with homelessness identified the provision of supported accommodation – or a greater quantity of supported accommodation – as one factor that could improve young people's housing situation. One officer expressed the need for support in the following terms:

> "That's part of the problem, you give a young person a set of keys, they may not have had the responsibility of looking after a tenancy in the past, and they get themselves into trouble, they just don't know what to do." (quoted in Harding, 1999, pp 64-5)

However, there is a lack of consensus about the specific needs that support is intended to meet – a point that is made in the context of single homeless people of all ages by Fitzpatrick et al (2000, p 48). Similarly, in the case of young people, McCluskey (1993, p 8) identifies a variety of roles that support may play:

> Support can range from practical help and advice on benefits, training and employment, to counselling to help to resolve emotional and relationship issues, and to life skills training to encourage the move to independence.

In addition to difficulties in defining support, there is a lack of evaluation of the types of support service that increase the likelihood of success in independent housing (Randall and Brown, 1994, p 7). As a result, services have sometimes been criticised as being based on incorrect assumptions about needs. In Kirby's (1994) study of care leavers, some respondents felt that the level and type of support provided in independent accommodation was inappropriate:

> So called 'supported independent accommodation' was not considered useful if it failed to meet young people's individual support needs, either because it did not offer enough responsibility or opportunities to learn practical skills, or if it had given them too much responsibility, without adequate support. (Kirby, 1994, p 20)

Fitzpatrick et al (2000, p 41) argue that funding conditions have sometimes forced the definition of support to be 'housing support', that is the encouragement of independent living skills (sometimes referred to as 'life skills'). Although there is no universally agreed list of such skills, a lack of them has often been given as a reason for difficulties in independent living. For example, in Harding's (1999) study, 12 of the 19 officers identified a lack of life skills as a problem for young people in their own accommodation: the abilities most frequently identified as lacking were looking after a property and buying and/ or cooking food.

A lack of budgeting skills is another factor frequently used to explain difficulties in independent living: agency workers in the study of Third et al (2001, p 17) argued that this was a reason for failure in young people's tenancies. Eleven of the officers in Harding's (1999, p 64) research identified budgeting as a skill lacked by some young people living independently. This problem was not usually seen as arising from a lack of income: only one officer identified a lower rate of benefit for the under 25s as contributing to difficulties. The reasons given for budgeting problems were more likely to focus on the irresponsible or immature attitude of the young person.

However, the belief that young people need assistance in the areas of budgeting and independent living skills in order to be successful in their own housing has been contested. Studies of young people have suggested that most do not perceive a need for help with life skills. Ainley's (1991, pp 108-9) study of 16-19 year-olds in independent housing found that, although undertaking domestic tasks was a frequently cited disadvantage of having their own property, most young people welcomed their new level of household responsibility and felt that they had matured as a result of it. In a study of 100 16- and 17-year-olds undertaken by Newcastle City Council (1994a), 96 said that they knew how to keep a home clean, 86 how to cook proper meals, 86 how to use a heating system and 66 what to do if there was a gas leak.

Hutson (1999, p 217) cites research which showed that – when asked about their own support needs – a minority of single homeless people requested assistance with sorting out benefits and budgeting, while only 8% asked for help with tasks such as cooking and shopping. Similarly, Fitzpatrick (2000, pp 124-5) found that less than half of her sample of young homeless people needed assistance with life skills. However, only seven of the 25 sample members said that they would prefer accommodation without support: they were most likely to express a need for help with budgeting and coping with bills (Fitzpatrick, 2000, p 125). In Anderson et al's (1993, pp 109-10) study of single homeless people, three fifths of the 16- and 17-year-old age group said that they would need help with housekeeping or money management: a higher figure than for the sample as a whole (Anderson et al, 1993, p 98).

So the balance of findings from research undertaken among young people suggests that many feel that they need assistance with budgeting, although less feel that life skills (however defined) are an area in which they need assistance.

Little attention has been paid to gender differences in discussions of the personal failings that are believed to lead to difficulties in independent living. Campbell (1993, pp 202-3) suggests that the inability to settle into an independent home is particularly likely to be a male problem, aggravated by unemployment:

> In employment, men's exit from the domestic domain was excused – they had to go out to work. In unemployment they have no alibi, their existence is domesticated.... In unemployment, men's flight from fatherhood has no hiding place, they have children and then leave someone else to look after them. What they all seem to insist upon, however, is that someone else should take care of them, too, that someone should take them in. Nothing in the culture these men make encourages them to take care of themselves, to create a domestic domain. Being a man means being not-a-woman. So, unable and unwilling to make homes of their own, they become cuckoos moving between their mothers and other women.

Elsewhere, Campbell (1984, p 57) argues that managing the family's finances has traditionally been the responsibility of women, while Finn (1984, p 50) found that young women in their final year of compulsory education were more likely than young men to undertake key jobs such as cooking and cleaning. So it may be that young men are particularly likely to need support with budgeting and independent living skills: an issue that will be returned to when considering the data collected for this study.

Structural failings

Campbell's argument about the effect of unemployment raises the issue of the influence of structural factors. She forcefully rejects the idea that financial difficulties on the part of people with low incomes should be attributed to a lack of budgeting skills:

> When you've lived on subsistence for two years what do you do when your shoes wear out, when you get a £100 fuel bill, when the washing machine breaks down, when a pair of children's shoes cost more than you'd spend on your own? Poverty makes economy impossible, not because the poor are improvident but because economy is always a matter of scale – bulk buying demands bulk incomes. (Campbell, 1984, p 17)

In the specific case of young people living independently, other writers have argued that it is their level of income, rather than the way that the money is used, that creates difficulties. Hutson (1999, p 220) argues that the main problem facing single homeless people – and the main reason why they fail in their tenancies – is a lack of money. She suggests that increasing a low income may be more important than tackling perceived personal inadequacies: an extra payment of £20 per week to a young homeless person may be a more cost-effective method of supporting them than maintaining a team of support workers at a cost of £350 per week. Similarly, while acknowledging that budgeting problems arose partly from inexperience, Fitzpatrick (2000, p 125) suggests that very low incomes were also part of the explanation of financial problems among her sample. The young people themselves thought that the factor most likely to resolve their difficulties was gaining access to employment and a reasonable income (Fitzpatrick, 2000, p 124).

It is frequently argued that young people living in their own housing experience a high degree of material hardship, although there is no direct evidence to link this hardship to the failure of tenancies. Third et al (2001, pp 10-11) list the following factors as being among the material disadvantages experienced by people aged 16-25 who are living independently: a lack of resources to decorate, inadequate furnishings, fuel poverty and difficulties in paying rent, Council Tax and Benefit Agency loan repayments.

A National Children's Home's (1993) study of 120 young people revealed even more striking difficulties. Two thirds of the sample were aged between 16 and 18 and almost all were living away from their families, most commonly in supported housing schemes or independent rented housing. Lack of money meant that one in three of the respondents had eaten only one meal, or no meal at all, during the previous 24 hours. Virtually all those interviewed, including the young women who were pregnant or mothers, did not eat sufficiently well to satisfy the World Health Organisation's criteria for a healthy diet. In addition, the sample tended to suffer from poor health, depression and low self-esteem (National Children's Home, 1993, p 3).

One key piece of legislation that is frequently linked to material hardship among young people is the 1988 Social Security Act, which ended the entitlement of 16- and 17-year-olds to Income Support. The Conservative government of the time claimed that young people were instead "guaranteed" a place on a Youth Training Scheme (Harris, 1989, p 144). However, concerns were subsequently expressed about the numbers of 16- and 17-year-olds not in work, education or training (for example, Social Security Advisory Committee, 1992, cited in Kay, 1994, p 5; MacLagan, 1993, p 13). More recently, the Social Exclusion Unit (2000a, p 18) suggested that one in eleven 16- and 17-year-olds were not involved in any form of 'economic' activity – and so at risk of having no income – at any one time.

In addition to a lack of material resources, agency workers in the study of Third et al (2001, p 17) identified another structural factor as contributing to the failure of young people's tenancies – feelings of isolation within low-demand neighbourhoods. Living in a disadvantaged area has often been linked to an increased risk of experiencing a number of social problems – for example, teenage pregnancy[4].

A high level of social problems on some local authority estates is sometimes blamed on a specific government policy measure, that is the 1980 Housing Act, which gave most long-standing local authority tenants the right to buy at a discount the property that they were living in. As council house sales rose after the passing of the 1980 Act, a process of residualisation began: a reduced social rented sector accommodated a higher concentration of low-income households (Malpass and Murie, 1994, pp 148-9). The right to buy left local authorities with a concentration of properties in less sought after areas. Properties in the inner or outer suburbs were most likely to be purchased, with inner-city and peripheral estates remaining predominantly under local authority ownership (Forrest and Murie, 1990, p 108).

Jones and Murie (1998, pp 626-7) note that the purchasing of properties by more affluent tenants left council housing with a narrower social base, consisting largely of low-income tenants who were dependent on Social Security benefits. They suggest that the concentration of disadvantaged households on local authority estates contributed to a spiral of neighbourhood decline.

As 16- and 17-year-olds are unlikely to be able to purchase their own property or to rent from other landlords, those who live independently are particularly likely to experience the effects of the residualisation of local authority housing. However, there has been only limited discussion of their experience of living in difficult areas. Harding (1999, p 63) found that local authority officers working in metropolitan areas reported difficulties for young people not so much in finding accommodation as in being able to live with any degree of comfort once in it. These difficulties arose from social problems such as crime. Other research has suggested that young people attach great importance to living in an area free of major social problems: Hutson (1999, pp 214-5) notes the importance of being rehoused into a property that is "quiet" while Fitzpatrick

(2000, p 36) found that safety was the most important factor in young people's definition of home.

Third et al (2001, p 51) also found that young people expressed a wish to be rehoused into a "decent" or "quiet" area and argue that:

> One of the most striking findings emerging from the consultation with young people was the impact of the area in which they lived on their ability to sustain tenancies. (Third et al, 2001, p 94)

So structural explanations of difficulties in independent living can concentrate on either the economic circumstances of the individual or the concentration of problems in a geographical area. These two elements are linked together in the concept of social exclusion – the Labour government's favoured explanation of social problems, which will be discussed further in the next chapter.

Failings in informal support

Turning to the final explanation for difficulties in independent living, some advocates of support have suggested that it is needed to make good a shortfall in the care provided by a young person's family. For example, Darke et al (1992, p 33) argue that:

> Having sufficiently urgent needs to be re-housed as homeless does not guarantee that a young person knows how to manage a tenancy. The family that forces a young person to leave may also have failed to teach them the necessary lifeskill.

One strand of evidence to support the view that family background is linked to difficulties in independent living is the high risk of homelessness faced by care leavers (see, for example, Hutson and Liddiard, 1994, p 60; DoH, 1999, p 15)[5]. Some writers (for example, Murray, 1990; Dennis and Erdos, 1993; Murray, 1994) have suggested that being brought up by a lone parent also increases the risk of experiencing social problems.

Taking a broader view, agencies in the study of Third et al (2001, p 17) viewed problems with families, neighbours or peer groups as factors contributing to failure in tenancies among young people. The agencies argued that there was a need for "befriending" services to combat the isolation that some young people experienced (Third et al, 2001, p 12).

However, there is also evidence to suggest that most young people who have left home at an early age are likely to continue to receive support from their families. Borland and Hill (1996-97, pp 60-1) found that even teenagers in the most tense family relationships desired continuing support. Jones (1995, p 90) and Fitzpatrick (2000, p 91) both found that leaving home often improved the relationship that young people had with their parents. In the study of Allen and Dowling (1998, p 66), young lone mothers living independently received substantial support from their own parents, although a less favourable picture emerged from the research of Speak (1995).

The type of support provided may not be financial: Fitzpatrick (2000, p 92) found that it was emotional support that was most likely to be provided by the families of her sample of young homeless people. Jones (1995, p 84) showed that access to continuing financial support after leaving the family home depended partly on the economic position of the family. There may also be gender differences in the level of support available: Smith et al (1998, p 37) found that young men who had left home experienced particular difficulties in re-establishing family relationships if they had had a confrontational relationship with their father or stepfather.

The role played by peer groups – in young people's experience of independent tenancies and their transition to adulthood more generally – is an underresearched area. MacDonald and Marsh (2002, pp 11-14) identify the role that a peer group can play in either encouraging or discouraging a young person to take drugs or commit crimes. Their research showed that new friends could be a major factor leading to a move away from such activities:

> ... a change in peer group associations could place individuals in situations where previously valued identities and activities no longer held status. Such changes were sometimes motivated by a housing move from one estate to another, by the establishment of new friendship groups through participation in, for instance, a training scheme or by a simple choice to associate with a different group. (MacDonald and Marsh, 2002, p 14)

The present study indicates that friends also have a substantial impact on young people's experience of independent living, as will be discussed in subsequent chapters.

Themes for analysis

The research described in this book examines the experiences of a sample of 16- and 17-year-olds rehoused as homeless in Newcastle upon Tyne (the city is referred to from here as Newcastle). It considers which of the three explanations of difficulties mentioned earlier is most helpful in explaining why some of the sample 'succeeded' in independent tenancies while others failed.

Gender differences are a major theme of the discussion – this issue is underdeveloped in all three explanations. Structural explanations include some discussion of differences between the employment difficulties of young men and young women (see, for example, Ashton et al, 1990, pp 50-1). In addition, there is limited discussion within both explanations that blame individual failings, and those that blame shortcomings in informal support, of difficulties that young men are more likely to face. This study examines in more detail gender differences in the experience of independent living[6].

Another key aim of this book is to evaluate relevant policies of central and local government – the central government approach to young people living independently is the subject of the next chapter.

Notes

[1] Similar measures had been implemented in Wales under the 2001 Homeless Persons (Priority Need) (Wales) Order (Welsh Statutory Instrument 2001 No 607 [W.30]). The Scottish Executive passed the Homelessness (Scotland) Bill in March 2003, phasing out the distinction between priority and non-priority homeless households by 2012, with the intention of ensuring that all unintentionally homeless households were entitled to permanent accommodation (Scottish Executive, 2003).

[2] The term 'household' refers to the homeless applicant and anyone who could reasonably be expected to live with them.

[3] The phrase '16-18 year olds' is used in many policy documents to cover young people from their 16th until their 18th birthdays. In this book, the phrase used is '16- and 17-year-olds, that is young people who would give their age as either 16 or 17.

[4] The Social Exclusion Unit (1999a, p 22) noted that there was not an exact match between deprivation and rates of teenage pregnancy. However, areas with concentrations of disadvantage and poverty dominated its list of the 10% of local authorities with the highest rate of conceptions among women aged 15-17.

[5] Other disadvantages faced by care leavers that have been highlighted by the government include up to 75% leaving care with no qualification and up to 50% becoming unemployed (DoH, 1999, p 15).

[6] It will be shown in Chapter Three that the data did not permit an investigation of racial differences.

TWO

Central government policy: from 'perverse incentives' to social exclusion

The present Labour government appears committed to tackling the difficulties experienced by young people living in independent housing, although it has not clearly identified which of the explanations of problems discussed in the first chapter it considers to be most significant. An examination of its approach reveals both similarities and differences with the policies adopted by previous Conservative administrations. While there has been a continuing emphasis on the responsibility of the individual to take work and training opportunities, a greater willingness to support young people in independent tenancies marks a major departure from the agenda of the Conservatives.

The Conservative legacy: removing 'perverse incentives'

The Conservative governments of 1979-97 had a clear objective of discouraging young people from moving into their own property before they were financially independent. This was part of a broader social policy agenda: Margaret Thatcher and the 'New Right' are widely assumed to have destroyed a post-war cross-party consensus over the role that the welfare state should play (Pierson, 1998, p 18). The Thatcher governments argued that the state had become too protective, reducing the incentive for individuals to provide for themselves. Their approach drew on anticollectivist ideas that public provision of benefits and services creates dependency and irresponsibility, rather than initiative, self-reliance and other desirable values (George and Wilding, 1985, pp 40-1). In addition to a greater emphasis on the responsibility of the individual to provide for themselves, the New Right also envisaged a greater role for the family: Harris (1988, p 502) notes that cuts to the benefits available to young people in the 1980s were linked to demands that their families shoulder more of the financial burden.

On the specific issue of young people living independently, the Conservatives sought to eliminate the perceived incentives to leave the family home needlessly and become financially dependent on the state. In particular, ministers argued that the homelessness legislation provided a reason for young women to have illegitimate children and so place themselves in a priority need category. Secretary of State for Wales John Redwood complained that there was a widespread belief among the young that "the illegitimate child is the passport to a council flat and benefit income" (*The Independent*, 14 August 1995, quoted in Jones and Novak, 1999, p 13). Similarly, Junior Health Minister Tom Sackville wrote in *The Observer* (14 November 1993, quoted in Jones and Novak, 1999, p 13) that the availability of benefits and council housing meant that "anyone can have a baby at any time, regardless of their means and of the circumstances in which they can bring up their babies".

Evans (1999, p 134) suggests that these concerns were an unstated reason for measures included in the 1996 Housing Act that weakened the protection available to homeless households:

> Notions of who most and least deserved social housing formed a critically important backcloth to the government's plans to reform the legislation, although they were not explicitly given as the reasons for changes. For example, there were a number of ministerial condemnations of young women becoming pregnant in order to qualify under the homelessness legislation, but these were usually voiced as part of a broader ideological campaign aimed at stemming the dependency culture and encouraging families to shoulder more of the welfare burden. The government's official justification for the legislation focused on issues of housing need.

This 'official' justification first appeared in a Consultation Paper preceding the Act, which argued that the existing homelessness legislation disadvantaged people in housing need who were prepared to wait on waiting lists (DoE, 1994, pp 3-4). Under the 1996 Act, local authorities no longer needed to secure permanent housing for households who were statutorily homeless[1]. Instead, they could discharge their legal duty by two methods: where there was suitable alternative accommodation available, only advice and assistance to access that accommodation needed to be provided. Alternatively, where suitable alternative accommodation was not available, the authority's obligation was to provide temporary accommodation and to allow the household to compete with others on the housing register for offers of permanent accommodation.

A desire to discourage inappropriate behaviour was made more explicit when cutting the benefits available to young people. Minister for Social Security Nicholas Scott argued that:

> Our policy is the correct one for the vast majority of 16-17 year olds; it would be irresponsible to provide a perverse incentive for people of this age to leave home needlessly. (DSS, 1989)

An example of such a perceived 'perverse incentive' was highlighted in 1984, when the government claimed that there was "public concern" over young unemployed people staying for extended periods in hotels and guesthouses in seaside resorts. Its response was to introduce time limits for which people under the age of 25 could be paid board and lodging rates of benefit to meet the cost of this type of accommodation: these limits were thought to represent the amount of time for which it was reasonable to stay in an area looking for work (Harris, 1989, pp 78-9).

The raising of the minimum age of entitlement to Income Support from 16 to 18 through the 1988 Social Security Act was intended to reduce incentives both to leave home and to be idle. Killeen (1988, p 24) notes that:

> The Government has justified Section 4 [of the 1988 Social Security Act] by suggesting that young people are refusing places on the Youth Training Scheme principally in order to claim Income Support. Lord Young, the Minister for Employment, has headed up a chorus of Government spokesmen deploring those idle young people who lie in bed all day rather than look for work.

Another measure that made leaving home more difficult was the creation by the 1986 Social Security Act of the Department of Social Security Social Fund. This replaced a system of single payments for 'one-off' expenses to households in receipt of means-tested benefits. In 1982 more than half of these single payments were for furniture and bedding (Craig, 1992, p 29). The changes that were brought about by the creation of the Social Fund were that payments became discretionary rather than based on entitlement, the budget for payments was cash limited and most payments were in the form of a loan rather than a grant (Andrews and Jacobs, 1990, pp 241-3). Evaluations of the Social Fund (for example, Stewart and Stewart, 1991; Petch et al, 1994) suggested that many people were unable to obtain assistance from it to furnish a new home.

The Conservatives also sought to discourage young people from leaving home prematurely through the provision of education. The Department of the Environment's (1991) Code of Guidance on Part 3 of the 1985 Housing Act presented education as a means of informing young people about the risk of homelessness that they faced. It argued that education was:

> ... crucial to help young people with independent living, and to ensure that they are aware of the risks of homelessness. Housing authorities should therefore liaise closely with local education authorities to get schools to include projects on housing and homelessness in their curricula. (quoted in Gholam, 1993, p 2)

The Conservative belief that individuals and their families should be responsible for their own welfare appeared not to extend to care leavers: the 1989 Children Act introduced a number of measures to support this group. Section 24 placed a duty on social services departments to "advise, assist and befriend" young people aged 16 to 21 who had previously been in public care. The guidance accompanying the Act referred to assistance in the provision of accommodation where the young person was not able to return home, single and homeless, young and roofless, a lone mother or with physical or learning disabilities

(Strathdee, 1993, p 14). Duties were also placed on local authorities, voluntary organisations and those running registered children's homes to advise, assist and befriend young people in their care with a view to promoting their welfare once they left. Guidance from the Department of Health indicated that part of young people's preparation for leaving care should be teaching them 'life skills' such as how to budget, shop, cook, find a flat, get a job and apply for benefits (Ryan, 1999, pp 222-3).

Another development that appeared to depart from the Conservative government view that young people should not be supported to live independently was the support that it gave to the foyers initiative. Foyers differ from other hostels in providing on-site assistance to access work and training opportunities (Gilchrist and Jeffs, 1995, p 4). The Employment Department expressed a belief that foyers could achieve a number of objectives, such as providing a safe place to go when young people first left home in search of a job and independence; giving expert information and training in a wide variety of areas; giving an opportunity to develop the skills and earning power needed for living independently; and providing an environment that was encouraging and conducive to work (Fordham, 1993, p 17, cited in Gilchrist and Jeffs, 1995, p 5)[2]. Between 1992 and 1998, 75 foyers were developed in the UK (Foyer Federation, 1998). An early evaluation of pilot foyer projects (Quilgars and Anderson, 1995) suggested that they could achieve some positive outcomes in terms of settling young people into stable employment and housing.

So the Conservatives' policies sought to support care leavers in independent living and included some measures to enable young people living independently to provide for themselves financially. However, their main aim was clearly to discourage young people from leaving the family home if they could not be financially independent – an aim that was pursued through restrictions to benefit entitlements and reductions to the protection provided by the homelessness legislation. A more complex picture emerges when considering the approach of the subsequent Labour governments.

New Labour

Current policies affecting 16- and 17-year-olds living in their own tenancies form part of the political approach associated with the 'New' Labour government – an approach that has been described as the 'Third Way'. Driver and Martell (2000, pp 148-9) argue that New Labour and the Third Way have often been defined negatively – that is, an approach that is neither New Right nor Old Left. However, there have been efforts to offer a positive definition – particularly influential in this area is Giddens (2000, pp 2-3), who argues that the Third Way is heavily influenced by the "new progressivism" of the Democratic Party in the United States:

> The cornerstones of the new progressivism are said to be equal opportunity, personal responsibility and the mobilising of citizens and communities. With

rights come responsibilities. We have to find ways of taking care of ourselves, because we can't now rely on the big institutions to do so. Public policy has to shift from concentrating on the redistribution of wealth to promoting wealth creation.

Taking the rights and responsibilities theme, a number of writers have noted the dual role that New Labour sees for the government and the individual in tackling social problems: individuals have rights to be given opportunities for advancement, but must act responsibly in taking these opportunities. Ellison and Pierson (1998, p 11) comment that the government wishes the worst off to become partners in its project – so long as they demonstrate that they are sufficiently committed to it. Heron and Dwyer (1999, p 92) echo this point, arguing that New Labour has promoted its ideas for the welfare state as a reciprocal arrangement, which imposes obligations on the individual as well as providing them with rights.

Consistent with the thinking of Giddens, the government has not overtly pursued a policy of redistributing income. Ellison (1998, p 41) argues that New Labour does not see its primary responsibility as being to improve the position of the poorest but rather to offer them opportunities to escape from their poverty. However, although Giddens (2000, p 53) argues that Third Way politics is more concerned with inequality of opportunity than inequality of outcome, he makes an exception where these unequal outcomes deny equal opportunities to future generations. Redistribution of wealth is necessary to re-allocate life chances (Giddens, 2000, p 89). The steps taken to improve the life chances of disadvantaged young people are discussed further later in this chapter.

The most important concept affecting the New Labour social policy programme – one that incorporates providing rights and responsibilities and ensuring equality of opportunity – is that of social exclusion. Giddens (2000, pp 104-6) argues that this term is intended to draw attention to the social processes that produce or maintain deprivation by denying some individuals the opportunities that are open to others. Some of these processes are structural, such as the decline in demand for male unskilled or semi-skilled labour (Giddens, 2000, p 104). Others are the result of the work of the welfare state itself, in producing poverty traps or housing estates with concentrations of deprivation (Giddens, 2000, pp 104-5). Exclusion on the worst estates or in the worst urban areas can take the form of physical separation from others, while in other cases it may mean lack of access to normal labour market opportunities (Giddens, 2000, p 105).

The government's definition of social exclusion is:

a shorthand term for what can happen when people or areas suffer from a combination of linked problems such as unemployment, poor skills, low incomes, poor housing, high crime, bad health and family breakdown. (SEU, 2001a, p 10)

The most important aspect of this definition is that the problems are linked and mutually reinforcing (SEU, 2001a, p 10). Past government policies have been blamed for failure to match rights and responsibilities, with a passive welfare state that sometimes trapped people on benefits rather than enabling them to help themselves (SEU, 2001a, p 27).

The government has taken an array of measures to tackle social exclusion, described in a series of reports produced by the Social Exclusion Unit, which was formed after the 1997 general election. However, despite the importance attached to it by the government, Ratcliffe (1998, pp 807-8) argues that social exclusion is a poorly constructed theoretical concept, which can define a fixed geographical location or examine the separation of the individual from mainstream society. The government acknowledges that its definition is deliberately flexible (SEU, 2001a, p 10).

Hills (2002, p 240) notes a further criticism of the concept of social exclusion – namely that it diverts attention from more controversial issues such as material deprivation, lack of income and redistribution. Although the government has discussed difficulties under headings such as "children living in low income households" (SEU, 2001a, p 17) and "workless households" (SEU, 2001a, p 18), it has not publicly advocated redistribution of income. However, a series of policies have resulted in gains for the poorest families with children, leading left-wing commentators to describe the government's approach as "doing good by stealth" (Lister, 2001, p 66).

A further criticism is that so many indicators of social exclusion have been developed that the government can claim progress by focusing on selected issues (Burchardt et al, 2002, p 42). This argument appears to be supported by an examination of the 2001 monitoring report on poverty and social exclusion of the New Policy Institute – an independent think tank. Fifty indicators of poverty and social exclusion were identified, of which seven related to young adults: unemployment (aged 16-24), on low rates of pay (aged 16-21), not in education, training or work (aged 16-18), problem drug use (aged 16-24), suicide (aged 15-24), without a basic qualification (aged 19), and with a criminal record (aged 18-21) (Rahman et al, 2001).

Leaving aside debates about definitions, some of the factors thought to contribute to the social exclusion of young people may be felt particularly acutely by those who are living independently. Lloyd's (1999) study of a sample of young men described as being "on the margins of social exclusion" showed that concerns about remaining in jobs with low pay and poor working conditions led some to improve their prospects by going to college. However, such a step was more difficult for those living away from their family home because of their immediate concerns with having the money to buy food and to pay rent and other bills.

The extent to which policies designed to tackle the perceived problem of social exclusion have assisted young people living in their own tenancies is a major theme of the research described in this book. These policies have both a personal and a geographical dimension. The government's approach to tackling the geographical elements of social exclusion were summarised in the Social Exclusion Unit's (2001b) National Strategy for Neighbourhood Renewal. High unemployment in particular geographical areas was to be tackled through the creation of action teams for jobs and employment zones. Initiatives to combat crime included the creation of crime and disorder reduction partnerships, a series of measures to combat antisocial behaviour, the funding and promotion of neighbourhood warden schemes and extra money to tackle drug problems. The problems of hard-to-let housing were to be relieved through regional strategies to tackle low demand and the unfreezing of the housing revenue account to ensure that there were more resources for housing management (SEU, 2001b, pp 34-41).

However, the major focus of policy has been attempts to tackle social exclusion at the level of the individual. Analysis of the initiatives taken for children and young people demonstrates the strong influence of the two principles discussed earlier: preventing inequality in life chances and combining rights with responsibilities.

New Labour's policies for young people

Although recent policies designed to re-allocate life chances were mainly implemented too late to benefit the sample chosen for this research, they are discussed briefly here because they may affect young people living independently in the future. The Prime Minister made a key policy commitment in 1999, when he pledged the government to eliminate child poverty within two decades (Lister, 2001, p 65). Official figures from April 2001 suggested that 500,000 children had been lifted out of poverty since the 1997 election, although the government prediction had been 1.2 million (*The Guardian*, 12 April 2002, p 8)[3].

Programmes have been devised to provide services to disadvantaged children and young people of all ages. In neighbourhoods where there is a high percentage of children living in poverty, Sure Start programmes have been introduced to improve services to families with children under the age of 4 (*The Guardian, Society*, 6 December 2000, p 6). A Children's Fund has been created to prevent poverty and disadvantage among children aged 5 to 13 (SEU, 2001a, p 37) and the Connexions Service has been introduced for 13- to 19-year-olds, providing personal advisers to give support in learning and in society more generally (SEU, 2001a, p 71).

The two primary aims of the Connexions Service are improving education achievement and increasing participation in education and training (SEU, 2001a, p 71). The number of 16- and 17-year-olds not participating in work, education or training was noted in the previous chapter: improving opportunities in these areas has been a major concern of government policy.

The Conservatives had already sought to modernise training through the introduction of Modern Apprenticeships in 1995-96. Labour has gone further by introducing National Traineeships and Other Training, which replaced Youth

Training (the successor to the Youth Training Scheme) from April 1998. National Traineeships and Modern Apprenticeships aim to provide young people with qualifications at levels two (equivalent to GCSE), three (equivalent to A level) or above. In 1998-99 there were 134,600 young people on Modern Apprenticeships, 120,500 on Other Training and 30,400 on National Traineeships (ONS, 2003a).

The Social Exclusion Unit's report on 16- and 17-year-olds not in education, employment or training promised the funding of new education and training opportunities for young people not suited to standard provision (SEU, 1999a, p 94). One measure that implemented this pledge was the introduction of the Learning Gateway in September 1999. The Gateway seeks to bring back into mainstream learning two groups of 16- and 17-year-olds: those who are disaffected by attitude – for example, as a result of school exclusion or low levels of school achievement – and those who are disadvantaged by circumstances or characteristics, such as homelessness, a care history, family difficulties or offending behaviour. A Life Skills programme helps some of these young people to develop self-esteem and motivation before moving onto a training course or further education (QPID, 2000).

More recently, the government has introduced an entry to employment programme for those young people who are not yet ready to take up Modern Apprenticeships or other work-related learning (Learning and Skills Council, 2003, p 6). The learning objectives for the programme include improving motivation and confidence, developing basic and/or key skills, and acquiring knowledge, skills and understanding through opportunities to sample different work and learning contexts (Learning and Skills Council, 2003, p 11).

In order to encourage young people from low-income families to continue in education, the government has introduced pilot schemes of education maintenance allowances (EMAs). These are provided in full to 16- and 17-year-olds who are in full-time education and whose parents earn less than £13,000 per year (SEU, 1999b, p 75). At the time of writing, the government is planning to expand this scheme nationwide after pilot projects indicated that allowances could increase the number of children who stayed on at school after 16 by 5%. In the most disadvantaged areas, where teenagers were receiving the highest payments, the figure was 11% (*The Observer*, 2 June 2002, p 2).

The Social Exclusion Unit (2001a, p 33) has identified the provision of EMAs – which are conditional on students reaching certain levels of attendance and performance – as an example of a policy balancing rights and responsibilities. The government's enthusiasm for the allowances was demonstrated by a pledge to establish a set of pilot projects to examine the extra support (in addition to EMAs) that would enable homeless 16- and 17-year-olds to remain in education (SEU, 1999b, p 98).

In contrast to its desire to support young people who are willing to meet their responsibilities to take up education or training opportunities, the government has given no indication that it intends to restore an entitlement to means-tested benefits for 16- and 17-year-olds. There remain limited circumstances in which a 16- or 17-year-old may be able to claim the key benefits of Income Support and income-based Jobseeker's Allowance (JSA)[4]. JSA may be payable if a young person is forced to live away from their parents and would suffer severe hardship if not paid benefit, or if they are a member of a couple responsible for a child (DWP, 2003a). Income Support may be paid to 16- and 17-year-olds who are still in education, if they are parents, severely disabled, orphaned or – in certain circumstances – if they are living away from parents or carers. If not in full-time education, the circumstances under which non-disabled 16- and 17-year-olds without children can receive Income Support are extremely limited (DWP, 2003b).

The Social Exclusion Unit (2000a, p 78) has recommended research to establish how effective Jobseeker's Allowance Severe Hardship Payments and Income Support are in meeting the needs of vulnerable 16- and 17-year-olds. However, the main concern of the government is undoubtedly to extend rights to the young people who are prepared to meet their responsibilities by taking up education or training places.

New Labour and independent living

The government has suggested that its policies on social exclusion will help to prevent homelessness (DTLR, 2002a, p 18)[5]. For some of the policies identified as being effective in this area – particularly the Sure Start programme and the Children's Fund (DTLR, 2002b, p 45) – the main beneficiaries are likely to be parents (including young lone parents) and their dependent children. In the case of childless young people, the government has indicated that the Connexions Service can help to meet the needs of those with housing difficulties:

> … the personal adviser, in partnership with other workers, will need to help
> the young person find and settle in suitable accommodation, or help them
> to return safely to the family home, to enable them to successfully engage in
> learning and work. (DTLR and Connexions, 2001, p 13)

The government has further emphasised the importance of 'economic' activity by suggesting that education, training and employment can help to protect young people against homelessness (DTLR and Connexions, 2001, p 12). A similar emphasis is evident in its strategy on rough sleeping, which states that:

> It is vital that we never give up on routing people into education, training
> and employment as a way of ensuring they are full and equal members of
> our society. It is also vital that we provide the stepping stones required for
> those people who need extra help to get there. (Rough Sleepers Unit,
> 2001, p 18)

The strategy discusses a pilot scheme in Nottingham, aimed at encouraging young homeless people – or young people at risk of homelessness – to enter, and remain in, further education (Rough Sleepers Unit, 2001, p 21). Elsewhere, foyers and other schemes that combine accommodation with employment and training opportunities have been identified as being particularly suitable for some young people (DTLR, 2002b, p 65). The number of foyers has continued to grow under the Labour governments, reaching 114 by early 2002 (*Inside Housing*, 25 January 2002, p 16).

In addition to the support for foyers, continuity of approach is also evident in concerns that the government has expressed about young people leaving home prematurely:

> All agencies providing accommodation and services for homeless young people should give priority to trying to prevent them from becoming homeless, rather than the automatic provision of accommodation. Housing young people before they are able to sustain independent living is likely to lead to the breakdown of the tenancy and can lead to long term homelessness. Where young people have a family home to which they could safely return, this should be the preferred option, as it is better for the long term stability of young people to leave home in a planned way than in a crisis. (DTLR, 2002b, p 46)

The government has encouraged the provision of education about the risk of homelessness in schools and has emphasised that the aim of such education should be "sustaining young people in their homes, rather than encouraging too early independence" (DTLR, 2002b, p 46). Family mediation services have also been supported, in the belief that they can prevent young people from leaving home at an inappropriate time:

> In many cases the use of home visits and the availability of mediation services can help to reconcile families and friends and prevent homelessness from occurring.... (Homelessness Directorate, 2003, p 9)

However, the current government does not appear to share the concern of the Conservatives that overgenerous service provision for those living in their own tenancies can create 'perverse incentives' to leave the family home. Instead it has taken a number of measures to address the needs of young people who are living independently.

The most obvious indication of this different approach has been changes to the homelessness legislation, where the protection available to homeless households has been strengthened. Under the 2002 Homelessness Act, local authorities can no longer meet their legal obligations to statutorily homeless households by satisfying themselves that there is suitable alternative accommodation available or by providing temporary accommodation. Instead they must secure an offer of suitable permanent accommodation. The government has extended the priority need categories to include 16- and 17-year-olds (as discussed in the last chapter), care leavers and people who are vulnerable because they have an institutional background.

Although its focus is on achieving economic independence, the government has acknowledged the need for a variety of support services for vulnerable people who are seeking to live independently. It has argued that effective support can reduce tenancy breakdown to very low levels and has identified a range of services that can help to resettle a formerly homeless person into independent accommodation. Although not specific to young people, the services discussed cover all three of the reasons for difficulties in independent tenancies that were discussed in the previous chapter. In the area of personal shortcomings, services include help with money management, resolving disputes with neighbours or the landlord and "ensuring that the tenant understands their rights and responsibilities, particularly the payment of rent" (DTLR, 2002b, p 39). The social/emotional support advocated includes help to integrate into the local community and "basic help with personal and emotional problems" (DTLR, 2002b, p 39) (the role that would often be played by family). In the area of material needs, the favoured services are help with moving in, furnishing the home and claiming welfare benefits. Unsurprisingly, help to access education, employment and training is also mentioned (DTLR, 2002b, pp 39-40).

When considering support needs that are specific to young people who must live independently, the government has argued that homelessness can be prevented by life skills training and a "reality check" to ensure that they understand the difficulties associated with finding and keeping accommodation (DTLR, 2002b, p 47). Similarly, it has suggested that Connexions personal advisers should provide young people living independently with "help with lifeskills such as budgeting", although assistance with benefit applications is also discussed (DTLR and Connexions, 2001, p 12). So it would appear that the emphasis on providing services to overcome personal shortcomings is particularly strong in the case of young people.

Two groups of young people who have been the subject of specific Labour government intervention in the area of independent living are care leavers and teenage parents. Measures to improve services to care leavers were proposed in the Green Paper *Me, survive out there?* (DoH, 1999) and implemented by the 2000 Children (Leaving Care) Act.

It might be assumed that the greatest difficulty faced by care leavers is a lack of family support, as they have been unable to live with their parents. However, the Green Paper identified difficulties they might experience in independent tenancies that could be linked to both material need and personal failings. The material factors included a lack of financial support, benefit dependency and an unsatisfactory housing situation. A key difficulty was thought to be an increasing trend to discharge young people from care at the age of 16 – compared to an estimated average age of leaving home of 22 for other young people (DoH, 1999, pp 13-14). Support was thought necessary to overcome the inexperience that could make independent living at such an early age problematic:

> They [care leavers] often have specific needs for support to help them to make the transition to living independently and to manage practical issues such as rent payment. (DoH, 1999, p 14)

The Act introduced a number of measures to strengthen the support provided both before and after young people left public care. To ensure that there was no financial incentive to discharge them at an early age (see DoH, 1999, p 18), 16- and 17-year-old care leavers were no longer able to apply for non-contributory benefits; instead local authorities were made responsible for meeting their financial needs from ring-fenced funds (DoH, 2001). In addition, Section 23B (8) created further responsibilities for local authorities towards young people in their care up until they were 18 – to provide them with (or maintain them in) suitable accommodation and to give other prescribed forms of support. These new responsibilities meant that the subsequent change to the homelessness legislation, placing 16- and 17-year-olds into the priority need category, did not affect young people in public care (although homeless care leavers aged 18-21 benefited from being placed in the priority need category).

The 2000 Children (Leaving Care) Act also required local authorities to assess the needs of each 16- or 17-year-old in their care and to provide a young person's adviser (DoH, 2001). A key duty was to form Pathway Plans, providing a route to independence, including a consideration of when a young person might be ready to leave care (DoH, 2001). Elsewhere, the government has argued that:

> Housing plans and the prevention of homelessness will clearly be central to the Pathway Plans. (DTLR, 2002b, p 48)

In addition to care leavers, the present government also shares with its Conservative predecessors a particular concern for young lone parents, although these concerns have been expressed in less punitive terms than those used by Conservative ministers. The Social Exclusion Unit's report on teenage pregnancy (1999a, pp 91-102) included large numbers of recommendations for prevention but also identified measures to tackle exclusion among teenagers who had become pregnant. These recommendations included providing education maintenance allowances and childcare for 16- and 17-year-old mothers and changing the type of housing available to this group:

> By 2003, all under 18 teenage lone parents who cannot live with family or partner should be placed in supervised, semi-independent housing with support, not in an independent tenancy. (SEU, 1999a, p 102)[6]

The reason for this recommendation appeared not to be a wish to provide a disincentive to young, single women to become pregnant, but a concern to prevent social isolation. The report argued that living in a flat on her own with a young child could be an isolating experience for a young mother (SEU, 1999a, p 65). Elsewhere, the government has criticised previous approaches in the following terms:

> Teenage mothers were often forgotten by the education system, and propelled into life on their own rather than into supported housing, and without childcare to allow them to go back into learning or a job.   (SEU, 2001a, p 27)

The government has listed the elements that could go into a support plan for a young lone parent, depending on the capacities of the individual. Issues to be covered could include parenting skills, independent living skills, childcare, health promotion, assertiveness and self-esteem, training and education opportunities, and family and peer support (DTLR and Teenage Pregnancy Unit, 2001, p 15). Suggested approaches by which supported housing projects can develop independent living skills include cleaning rotas, staff escorting residents on shopping trips, assistance with menu planning and budget training that incorporates payment of the service charges (DTLR and Teenage Pregnancy Unit, 2001, p 17).

The approach to lone parents appears to reflect broader themes of government policy: tackling social exclusion; providing rights for young people prepared to accept their responsibilities to engage in work, education or training; and providing support aimed predominantly at overcoming personal shortcomings. As teenage parents with childcare responsibilities are almost invariably women, the development of services for them can be seen as a gender-specific policy. However, most policy for young people – like explanations of difficulties in independent tenancies – has been developed in a 'gender blind' manner. The data discussed in the next chapter will suggest that the failure to acknowledge gender differences is a major shortcoming of both academic debate and government policy.

Strategic thinking

Another key element of the current government's approach has been to ensure that support services to people living independently are delivered in a coordinated manner, with strategic planning provided by local authorities. It has frequently been argued in the past that a lack of coordination had reduced the effectiveness of services for vulnerable people in general (for example, Cameron et al, 2001) and young people in particular (for example, Roaf and Lloyd, 1995). The government has pledged to "join up" policy at national level and to ensure that authorities do the same at local level (DTLR, 2002a, p 19).

Sections 1-3 of the 2002 Homelessness Act placed an obligation on local housing authorities to form a homelessness strategy for their district. One of the aims of this strategy must be to ensure that support is provided to people who are or may become homeless, or who have been homeless in the past. The government has suggested that separate youth homelessness strategies could be integrated into wider homelessness strategies (DTLR, 2002b, p 44) – a further indication that it believes that young people have specific support needs in independent tenancies.

Local authorities are also required to form strategies to implement the government's Supporting People programme, which is the mechanism for planning and providing support to vulnerable groups living in their area. In order to create this strategy, authorities must undertake a needs map of housing support required by groups such as people leaving prison or women fleeing domestic violence. This should be compared to a supply map, showing the provision of housing-related support services. Existing quality services should then be developed and improved further, and some provision refocused on unmet need (DETR, 2001, pp 19-21).

The government has acknowledged that there will be overlapping and common features within homelessness and Supporting People strategies. Support services for homeless people are intended to be fully integrated with the local Supporting People policy (DTLR, 2002b, p 10). In discussing the services that might be provided to young homeless people through the Supporting People programme, the government has again demonstrated its view that personal inadequacies are the main difficulty to be overcome:

> Young homeless people, often with mental health or substance misuse problems, can find it very hard to hold down a tenancy or stay in one place long enough to get training, counselling, and other assistance in stabilising their lives. Supporting People provides the means of enabling them to settle into a new home, and learn basic life skills that other people take for granted like how to pay rent, shop for food, organise going to regular training and so on. This stable housing enables them to take the necessary steps forward towards independence and stability. (DETR, 2001, p 11)

Evaluating policy

Responsibilities to form homelessness and Supporting People strategies were not in place at the time of the research and so did not impact on the young people included in the sample. However, the research findings provide an important insight into the types of support need that should be met through these strategies. These issues will be considered further in Chapters Four and Five, which examine the impact of local authority policies on young people living independently. First the data are used to evaluate the government's view of the causes of social exclusion among young people living independently and the impact of the three types of difficulty discussed in the previous chapter.

In the area of structural difficulties, the data are used to assess the material conditions of 16- and 17-year-olds living in independent tenancies and the reasons for material hardship arising. A key element of Labour government policy is evaluated by examining the impact of participating in education or training – rather than receiving benefits – on the outcome of tenancies. The effect of the area in which a young person is rehoused is assessed in order to establish the appropriateness of measures taken by the government in its neighbourhood renewal programme.

Assumptions about young people's personal shortcomings – including their perceived lack of budgeting skills or 'life skills' – are assessed by considering the level of these skills among the sample and their impact on tenancy outcomes. A further assumption – that young people need warning about the difficulties associated with independent living – is evaluated by considering the extent to which the expectations of the sample about living in their own property were realistic, and whether unrealistic expectations could reduce the likelihood of a tenancy being successful. Particularly close attention is paid to the situation of care leavers and lone parents in order to establish whether the government's concentration of services on these two groups is appropriate. There is also consideration of the impact of young people's involvement in activities thought to contribute to social exclusion, such as crime and drug taking.

The impact of informal support is evaluated by examining the effect of receiving support from family and friends on the outcome of tenancies. There is also detailed consideration of the circumstances of groups who may be assumed to be socially isolated, particularly those who stayed in local authority temporary accommodation while awaiting permanent rehousing, in order to determine whether they have a particular need for support services.

The government has listed among its successes in tackling social exclusion: "16 to 18 year-olds getting the advice and support they deserve" (SEU, 2001a, p 4). The following chapters will examine the extent to which this boast is justified in the case of those who live in independent tenancies.

Notes

[1] This phrase refers to households who satisfy the four conditions discussed in the previous chapter – being homeless, not intentionally homeless, with a local connection and in priority need.

[2] It should be noted that this benign view of the role of foyers is not shared by all commentators: Gilchrist and Jeffs (1995, p 7) suggest that tying an offer of accommodation to a commitment to using job search facilities is similar to the conditions that were placed on residence in the workhouse.

[3] The same figures showed that 3,9 million children remained below the relative poverty line (*The Guardian*, 12 April 2002, p 8).

[4] They are unlikely to have been working for long enough to receive contribution-based Jobseeker's Allowance.

[5] Most of the documents cited in this section relate to services for homeless people, or to prevent homelessness. It was argued in the first chapter that much of the discussion of support needs in independent tenancies is in the context of preventing or tackling homelessness, although there may be young people with substantial needs who have never been homeless.

[6] This type of recommendation was also made by Hudson and Ineichen (1991, pp 214-15).

THREE

Young people's experience of independent tenancies

This chapter discusses the methodology employed in the research and the findings from interviews with young people living independently. In order to place the research into context, it is necessary to consider first the social and economic conditions that exist in Newcastle, particularly those that most affect young people.

Newcastle: the context

Census data for 2001 showed that 50% of people aged 16-74 were in employment in Newcastle, compared to an average for England and Wales of 60.6%. There were higher percentages of people in the city who were unemployed, economically inactive students or permanently sick or disabled than was the case nationally (ONS, 2003b). The government's (2000) indices of neighbourhood deprivation showed that, of 354 districts in England, Newcastle was the tenth most deprived in terms of employment and the eighteenth most deprived in terms of income (ONS, 2003b).

As might be expected from the economic profile of the city, there is a large social rented sector in Newcastle, with 33% of households living in this sector (ONS, 2003b), compared to 20% in England (Leather et al, 2002). As with other northern cities that lack job opportunities, the local authority has experienced difficulties with outward migration and falling demand for rented housing. The population of Newcastle fell by 16% between 1971 and 1996 (Power and Mumford, 1999) and there were 4,500 empty social rented properties in 2000 (NCC, 2000). A variety of social problems are evident in some areas where there is low demand for housing: for example, concentrations of poverty and unemployment, and a breakdown in informal social controls (Power and Mumford, 1999).

At the time when this research was conducted, the council's housing stock was divided into six management areas:

- Walker
- Gosforth, Byker, Heaton and Shieldfield
- Cruddas Park
- Blakelaw
- Benwell
- Newburn

Low demand was concentrated in the inner west areas of Cruddas Park and Benwell, although there were wards and neighbourhoods throughout the city that experienced problems.

Turning to issues that particularly affect young people, attendance at secondary schools in Newcastle was lower than the national average in 2001-02, as it had been in previous years (NCC, 2003a). In 2002, 38% of pupils passed five or more GCSEs with grades A★-C, compared to a national average of 52% (NCC, 2003b). Newcastle was in thirtieth position in the Social Exclusion Unit's (1999a, p 22) list of authorities with the highest rates of conceptions among young women aged 15-17.

The full range of responses of the local authority to poverty and disadvantage – particularly those aimed at young people living independently – will be considered further in the next chapter. One measure that is important to note here is that Newcastle decided in 1982 to accept all 16- and 17-year-olds as being in priority need under the homelessness legislation. The reasons that the local authority gave for adopting this approach were the particular vulnerability of this group [16- and 17-year-olds] in the housing market and the unsuitability of most of the single person hostels (NCC, 1983).

The research methodology and its rationale

Newcastle City Council commissioned the research described in this book largely because it had extensive experience of rehousing 16- and 17-year-olds as homeless, but only limited information about the factors that could make this rehousing successful. It was agreed that the research should take the form of a longitudinal study, examining the experiences of 16- and 17-year-olds in the year after their tenancy began. Previous research into youth homelessness has been criticised for being static in nature and for failing to predict the courses that young people's lives can take after their need has been identified (Fitzpatrick, 2000, pp 13-14). This research was intended to meet the need identified by Fitzpatrick and Klinker (2000) for longitudinal studies that track the progress of single homeless people and assess the effectiveness of interventions.

The potential sample for the study consisted of 16- and 17-year-olds who were accepted by the local authority as statutorily homeless and rehoused into permanent or semi-permanent accommodation. On approaching the homeless section, young people were invited to sign a consent form, indicating that an interviewer could visit to discuss their situation, and giving the researcher permission to collect information from other agencies about the support provided to them and the progress of their tenancy.

Those young people who signed the consent form and were subsequently rehoused,were visited by an interviewer in the early weeks of their tenancy. If the first interview was successfully completed, efforts were made to contact the young person after six months of their tenancy and conduct a further interview. Regardless of whether the attempt to conduct the first interview was successful, a number of agencies were asked to give information about any contacts that they had had with the young person.

Although the response rate was a little difficult to establish, it appeared that slightly less than half of the eligible 16- and 17-year-olds agreed to participate, in the 21-month period for which the study ran. The total number of respondents was 145 and 94 of this sample (64.8%) were interviewed at the first stage of the research. It became clear as the second stage of interviews progressed that there would be little success in trying to contact young people who had moved from their property and given a care-of address. After eliminating these respondents – and the ones who moved out leaving no forwarding address – there were 80 potential interviewees at the second stage. In 45 cases (56.3%) a second interview was completed. The discussion of the findings that follows refers to 145 young people in the case of information collected from agencies, 94 for data collected at the first interview and 45 for second interview data. Where comparisons are made between responses at the first and second interviews, these refer only to the 45 young people who gave a second interview.

The topics for the first interview schedule drew in part on the findings of a previous study conducted with young people living independently in Newcastle (Newcastle City Council, 1994a). Secondary analysis of the data collected for this study suggested that the following factors might influence whether a young person stayed in their tenancy or moved on:

- their gender;
- their perception of their money situation;
- their opinion of the area in which they lived;
- the frequency with which they saw their parents;
- whether they had been in care;
- whether they had children living with them;
- whether they had had advice about independent living;
- whether they felt that they had everything they needed;
- whether they had been in trouble with the police;
- their level of educational achievement.

In addition to covering these topics, the first interview in the present study asked young people to evaluate the services that they had received and to identify needs that they felt remained unmet. The second interviews established the changes that young people had experienced after six months and their view of moving into independent housing with the benefit of hindsight. Many of the questions asked at the second interview were identical to those in the first, in order to facilitate comparisons over time.

Turning to the evaluation of young people's experiences of independent living, this took place at two levels. The first was to investigate the incidence of long-term difficulties such as acquiring debts or being in trouble with the police in the course of a tenancy. The second was to judge the outcome of the tenancy from the perspective of the landlord. The adoption of the landlord's perspective was consistent with the discussion in the next chapter, which suggests that local authorities and housing associations increasingly have to justify initiatives in terms of improving the management performance of their organisation.

However, seeking to find indicators to measure 'success' in tenancies – even when using only the landlord's perspective – is not straightforward. Newcastle City Council itself has commented on the lack of consensus as to how to evaluate support services:

> ... it is hard to compare results and indeed it is hard to agree how to assess
> results at all. The single commonly agreed factor to emerge so far is length
> of tenure. (NCC, 1985)

Academic research has examined "tenancy sustainment" among young people (Third et al, 2001, p 9) and length of tenancy was the measure chosen by Harding and Keenan (1998) to demonstrate a housing management benefit from the provision of part-furnished tenancies in Newcastle. However, the need for a more complex measure in the present research was illustrated by one case of a young tenant who remained in their tenancy for six months – and so appeared to be 'succeeding' – but who had re-applied to the homeless section hoping to be offered another property, suggesting that their rehousing had been unsuccessful.

The criteria for measuring success and failure of tenancies were eventually decided after several informal consultations with housing professionals. To avoid over-reliance on one measure, three factors were used to indicate failure:

- terminating a tenancy in less than six months;
- terminating a tenancy in 6-12 months by means of abandoning the property, being evicted or leaving while awaiting eviction; or
- re-applying to the homeless section within 12 months of being rehoused.

Success in a tenancy was defined as having avoided all three of these negative outcomes.

One reason for choosing these criteria to measure success and failure was that fast turnover of tenancies, a property being abandoned or the tenant evicted, and repeated applications to the homeless section are all factors that impose financial costs on landlords. The other reason was that the criteria were all easily measurable: there was very little chance of the local authority making an error in recording the date on which the tenancy started and ended, whether a respondent had been evicted or abandoned their property, or whether they had subsequently been re-interviewed at the homeless section.

The interviews with the young people were structured, with all respondents being asked a standard set of questions. This approach – which facilitated quantitative analysis of the responses – had a number of advantages. It was possible to compare the percentage of sample members who smoked, for example, with national statistics collected by the Social Exclusion Unit (2000a). Where differences were observed between the sample and the national data, a statistical technique called the chi-squared goodness of fit test was used to measure the risk of concluding that these differences would still exist when considering all 16- and 17-year-olds rehoused as homeless in Newcastle at all times.

In addition, quantitative research is the method most commonly employed when seeking to establish causal relationships between concepts (Bryman, 1992, p 30). In contrast, qualitative research tends to pursue broader goals such as describing a social setting or viewing events from the perspective of the respondent (Bryman, 1992, pp 61-9). Demonstrating cause and effect between the outcome of tenancies and other variables appeared to be the approach most likely to ensure the provision, or continuation, of appropriate services to young tenants. It was anticipated that services that could be demonstrated to have a benefit in terms of tenancy outcomes would be developed further. Alternatively, the demonstration that an unmet need was having a negative effect might lead to services being introduced to meet that need.

One advantage of taking a large sample was that comparisons could be made between subgroups: for example, young men and young women, respondents with and without children. Differences between subgroups provided some of the most distinctive findings of the research and presented major challenges to policy makers, as will be seen in the discussion of the findings that follows.

Exact tests were the mechanism used for establishing whether a relationship between variables in the sample was likely to be replicated across all 16- and 17-year-olds rehoused as homeless in Newcastle at all times. For example, young people in the sample who had stayed in the local authority's temporary accommodation were less likely to succeed in their tenancy than those who had stayed temporarily with family or friends. This raised the question of whether the 22 sample members who had stayed in temporary accommodation were particularly prone to tenancy failure for other reasons, or whether the relationship between where a young person had stayed temporarily and the outcome of their tenancy would be reproduced in other samples at other times. The exact test gives a risk of error in adopting the latter explanation, for example, (p=0.01) means that there is only a 1% risk of error in assuming that there would be a relationship between the variables at all times. This figure is often referred to as the statistical significance of the findings. In this study, findings were not regarded as statistically significant if there was a greater than 10% risk of error (that is p>0.1) in assuming a relationship between the variables.

A further technique employed in this study was discriminant analysis, which is used when several independent variables have a statistically significant effect on a dependent variable. Discriminant analysis measures the correlations between the dependent variable and each of the independent variables, then ranks them according to which has the greatest effect. It was particularly important in this study to establish which variables most affected the outcome of tenancies.

The quantitative methods used raised many issues that could be examined further through in-depth interviews with young people living independently. For example, one variable that had a statistically significant effect on the outcome of tenancies was whether a sample member had ever taken drugs. This finding raised issues about the long-term effects of past events, and the role of the peer group, which could have been explored in more detail through qualitative interviews.

However, in moving into a new area of study, the main aim of the research was to identify those broad issues that had most bearing on young people's experience of independent living. Although using a 10% significance level – when many other studies prefer to use 5% – increased the risk of wrongly identifying a relationship between variables, it also increased the number of apparently significant relationships that could be explored through future research. The existing literature on youth homelessness includes many examples of qualitative research into more specific areas (for example, Kirby, 1994; Smith et al, 1998). It is hoped that the present study will be a starting point, stimulating more detailed examination of factors that appear to affect young people's experience of independent living and the outcome of their tenancies.

The sample, their rehousing and tenancy outcomes

Of the 145 16- and 17-year-olds who agreed to take part in the study, 107 (73.8%) were female and 38 (26.2%) were male. There were 17 respondents (11.7% – all of them young women) who had a child as part of their household at the time of applying to the homeless section: none had more than one. There were also 17 young women who said that they were pregnant when applying as homeless and two who said that they might be. When considering only those women who had no children and stated definitely that they were not pregnant, there remained a substantial gender imbalance in the sample: there were 71 women (65.1%), compared to 38 men (34.9%). The records of Newcastle's homelessness section show that this gender balance is representative of the 16- and 17-year-olds who have applied as homeless in recent years.

Previous studies (for example, Reid and Klee, 1999, p 19) have often assumed that young men make more use of conventional homelessness services because the dangers of sleeping rough mean that young women are more likely to find temporary accommodation with family and friends. However, this conventional wisdom is questioned by Fitzpatrick (2000, p 77), who argues that – in most cities – women form a slight majority of visibly homeless people; the reason for their apparent underrepresentation in some homeless services is that they may have children and so use services for homeless families instead. This study went further, suggesting that women formed a large majority of young people using homelessness services in Newcastle, even when excluding those who had children or were pregnant.

The ethnic origin of the respondent was recorded by staff at the homeless section in 101 cases; all 101 of these young people classified themselves as 'White – UK'. So although racial differences in housing circumstances generally (for example, Cameron and Field, 2000) – and in the housing circumstances of young people in particular (for example, Steele, 2002) – are widely acknowledged, they could not be examined by this study.

The majority of respondents (130 or 89.7%) were rehoused into self-contained local authority tenancies, although there were small numbers who moved into housing with more intensive support services (as is discussed further in the next chapter). Over half the sample was rehoused into high-rise or low-rise flats: other forms of accommodation included houses, maisonettes and bedsits.

According to the measure of success and failure discussed earlier, 76 of the 145 respondents (55.1%) were considered to have succeeded in their tenancies, while 62 (44.9%) failed. The number of respondents judged to have failed because of the reason that they terminated their tenancy was 30, although several of these also left the tenancy in less than six months or returned to the homeless section.

In total, 89 respondents (61.4%) left their original tenancy in the year after they were rehoused. The complete list of reasons for termination is shown in Table 3.1.

Respondents who had left their tenancy in the first six months were particularly difficult to find subsequently – only nine were interviewed at the second stage. Three had moved onto another tenancy of their own, while six had moved back to the home of their parent(s). Of the three respondents who had moved to another rented property, two said that they were now happier with their housing situation than they had been at the first interview, while one said that they felt about the same. Among the six who had returned to their parents, four felt happier now with their housing situation while two felt less happy. Given that respondents who left the property after less than six months were judged to have 'failed' in their tenancy, these findings illustrate that the definition of success and failure used in the research was based on the perspective of the landlord rather than that of the tenant.

Table 3.1: Reasons for terminating tenancies

Reason for leaving	Frequency	%
Flit	25	28.1
Domestic reasons	16	18.0
Transfer to other local authority accommodation	8	9.0
Fear of crime	6	6.7
Eviction	4	4.5
Burglary	3	3.4
Left while awaiting eviction	1	1.1
Other	25	28.1
Not known	1	1.1
Total	89	100.0

Structural factors and independent living

Material circumstances

Several variables demonstrated that the sample experienced severe material disadvantage. Table 3.2 shows the economic status of respondents at the time of the first interview.

As was noted in Chapter One, the Social Exclusion Unit (2000a, p 18) has estimated that one in eleven 16- and 17-year-olds (9.1%) are not in education, training or employment at any one time. In this sample – when excluding respondents with caring responsibilities, those who were long-term sick or disabled and the young woman who was on maternity leave – there were 46 young people (48.9%) who appeared to be without any form of 'economic' activity. The chi-squared goodness of fit test showed that there was a less than 0.1% risk of error in concluding that 16- and 17-year-olds rehoused as homeless in Newcastle are more likely to be unemployed than other people in the same age group.

The small numbers in work, education or training may have been a reflection of limited achievement at school: 52 first interview respondents (55.3%) had no GCSEs[1]. For a number of years, the percentage of young people in Newcastle who had not achieved any GCSE qualifications has been either 11 or 12% (NCC, 2003c). There is, therefore, a less than 0.1% risk of error in concluding that 16- and 17-year-olds rehoused as homeless in Newcastle are more likely to have left school without qualifications than other young people in the city.

As small numbers of the sample were working or on training schemes, it was unsurprising to discover that 41 first interview respondents (43.6%) identified Income Support as their first source of income. Weekly income levels were very low, with a mean figure of £43.74 and 55 first interview respondents

Table 3.2: Employment status of respondents at first interview

Status	Frequency	%
Registered unemployed	42	44.7
Government training scheme	13	13.8
At school	8	8.5
Attending college	7	7.4
Looking after home or family	7	7.4
Employed full time	5	5.3
Long-term sick or disabled	4	4.3
Employed part time	2	2.1
Receiving Income Support	1	1.1
Not registered as unemployed	1	1.1
Attempting to register as unemployed	1	1.1
Have appointment to make claim for benefit	1	1.1
On maternity leave	1	1.1
Not known	1	1.1
Total	94	100.0

(63.2%) receiving £40 per week or less. The five respondents who were working full time fared only slightly better – the highest weekly wage was £100 and the lowest only £60.

Most of the sample struggled to meet their weekly living expenses from their limited income. Only 12 first interview respondents (12.7%) said that their money always lasted until the end of the week, compared to 74 (79%) who said that it did not and six (6.4%) who did not yet know if this would be the case. In two cases (2.1%) the question was not applicable because the respondent had no income. Borrowing appeared to be a key method of coping with money running out: 53 first interview respondents (56.4%) said that they regularly borrowed money.

This picture of substantial financial difficulties was reinforced by respondents' assessment of their own money situation, as shown in Figure 3.1.

Consistent with the high level of material hardship among the sample was substantial experience of debt and, more strikingly, an increased likelihood of owing money after six months of independent living. There were 31 respondents (33%) who had debts at the time of the first interview. Money was most frequently owed to a parent or parents, but other common creditors were the council, friends, catalogues and other relatives. Respondents reported that

Figure 3.1: Respondents' assessment of their money situation: first interview

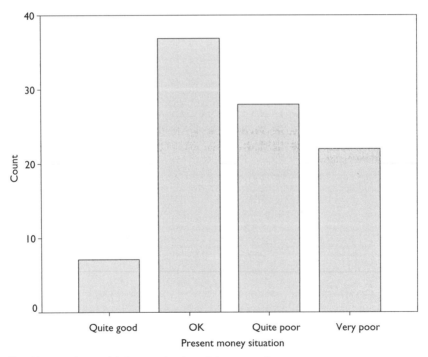

Note: No respondent rated their money situation as being very good.

various items of expenditure had caused the debts, most commonly general living, rent and clothes. By the time of the second interview, 30 respondents (66.7%) were in debt, compared to only 15 of the 45 (33.3%) who had been at the time of the first interview. Although a parent or parents were still a source of credit in eight cases, 15 respondents now owed money to the council and the incidence of catalogue debt had also increased.

The greater incidence of debt was the only major change to the sample's financial circumstances by the time of the second interview. Average income had risen to £54.98 per week, but this may have been because a number of respondents had become mothers in the time between the interviews (see later section). The number of respondents who were now registered unemployed was 21 (or 46.7%), compared to 20 at the time of the first interview. There had been small increases in the numbers who said that their money sometimes did not last until the end of the week and that they borrowed regularly.

In addition to demonstrating the persistence of material hardship, the data showed clearly that there were links between the financial situation of the young people and their assessment of their own health. When first interview respondents were asked about their general state of health, the responses were mainly positive: 56 (59.6%) said it was "very good" or "good", 31 (33%) replied that it was "okay" and only 6 (6.4%) said "poor" or "very poor". The sample's assessment of their health situation had statistically significant relationships with their weekly income ($p=0.041$), whether they regularly borrowed money ($p=0.012$) and how they rated their money situation ($p=0.055$). The most striking illustration of the relationship between material circumstances and perceived health was that only 24 of the 53 respondents who regularly borrowed money considered their health to be very good or good (45.3%), compared to 23 of the 28 respondents who did not regularly borrow (82.1%).

Half the first interview respondents did not eat a healthy diet. A more positive finding was that 85 (90.4%) had a GP, although some seemed to be making heavy use of this service: 26 (27.7%) had been to see a doctor at the surgery three times or more in the previous three months.

Reasons for material hardship

One issue that is frequently discussed in debates about poverty and low income is whether material hardship arises from inadequate resources or from frivolous spending on unnecessary items, particularly cigarettes (see, for example, Mack and Lansley, 1985, pp 117-27). Chapter One raised the question of whether young people in independent housing needed to be provided with a higher income or given budgeting advice to ensure that they used their limited resources to maximum effect. In order to explore this question further, first interview respondents were asked about their spending on alcohol, cigarettes and drugs. The answers given made possible the calculation of a composite spending figure for 86 respondents: in 30 cases (34.9%) this figure was less than £10 per week, in 29 (33.7%) it was £10-£20 and in 27 (31.4%) it was more than £20.

However, comparisons with the sample's reported income suggested that these figures should be treated with caution. Nine respondents appeared to have a negative weekly income after spending on alcohol, cigarettes and drugs, while five had an income of £5 or less. These young people – and seven who did not give a figure for their weekly income – were excluded from analysis comparing the likelihood of being in debt with spending on alcohol, cigarettes and drugs. The analysis showed that respondents who spent more than £10 per week on these items faced a greater risk of debt ($p=0.025$). In contrast, respondents who were in debt at the time of the first interview were not significantly more likely than others to have an income of £40 per week or less, to regularly borrow money or find that their money did not last until the end of the week, although they were more likely to perceive their own financial situation negatively ($p=0.012$).

The influence of spending on 'unnecessary' items was demonstrated further when examining a wide range of other first interview variables to establish whether they affected the likelihood of a respondent being in debt. Respondents were more likely to have debts at the time of the first interview if:

- they smoked daily ($p=0.012$);
- they were currently taking drugs ($p=0.001$);
- they had ever taken drugs ($p=0.043$);
- they had been in trouble with the police ($p=0.074$);
- they had stayed in local authority temporary accommodation ($p=0.05$);
- they expected to experience problems in independent living ($p=0.075$);
- they felt that their property was inadequately furnished ($p=0.082$); and
- they felt that they had not had enough advice about independent living ($p=0.012$).

Discriminant analysis showed that the four variables with the greatest influence over the likelihood of respondents being in debt were:

- whether they were taking drugs at present;
- whether they had stayed in local authority temporary accommodation;
- how often they smoked;
- weekly spending on alcohol, drugs and cigarettes.

The disadvantages experienced by the group of young people who had stayed in local authority temporary accommodation will be discussed in a later section. The other three variables clearly support the finding that it is primarily personal habits and individual spending patterns that increase the risk of debt for young people living independently, rather than low income or other material difficulties.

To examine whether different factors affected the acquisition of debts over a longer period of time, a new variable was created for the 30 second interview respondents who had not been in debt at the time of the first interview. This variable divided those who had fallen into debt by the time of the second interview from those who had not. Examination of the relationship between this 'new debt' variable and others from the second interview showed that respondents who had acquired debts since the first interview were more likely to now be regularly borrowing money ($p=0.023$). They were also more likely to say that not enough support was provided to young people in independent housing ($p=0.033$): this is similar to the finding at the first interview that respondents who were in debt were more likely to feel inadequately advised.

In addition, respondents who had acquired new debts since the first interview were particularly likely to say that they had experienced unexpected problems living in their own property ($p=0.086$), suggesting that they were unprepared for the financial difficulties that they had experienced. This view was supported by the finding that those respondents who had not expected difficulties in independent living at the first interview were particularly likely to have fallen into debt by the second ($p=0.086$). The links between feeling inadequately advised, being unprepared for difficulties in independent living and falling into debt clearly point to the need for financial advice at an early stage.

Another key finding about new debts concerned the links with particular geographical areas. Respondents who had been rehoused into the two lowest-demand areas of the city – Cruddas Park and Benwell – were particularly likely to have acquired debts in the six months between the interviews ($p=0.061$). Discriminant analysis showed that this variable had the greatest effect on the likelihood of falling into debt by the second interview. So, while many of the findings discussed earlier suggest that debts are often the result of inappropriate spending or being unprepared for independent living, the environment into which a young person is rehoused also seems to play a part.

Material circumstances and tenancy outcomes

Although the sample clearly suffered from substantial material hardship, this hardship had a limited impact on the outcome of tenancies. The only financial variable to have a statistically significant effect was whether, at the first interview, a respondent's money did not last until the end of the week ($p=0.037$) (see Table 3.3).

The limited evidence provided by the two respondents who had no income at the time of the first interview suggests a link between severe material hardship and tenancy failure. However, more difficult to explain is the reason for the young people who did not yet know whether their money would last until the end of the week succeeding in their tenancies. In one case the respondent said that they did not yet know because they had only just moved in, but the other five were still waiting to receive benefit payments. It appeared that these initial delays had a positive effect on the eventual tenancy outcome. The apparently beneficial effect of early difficulties in independent living was a theme that recurred throughout the analysis of the data.

Table 3.3: Cross table of whether tenancy successful by whether money sometimes does not last until end of week

| | | Tenancy successful? | | |
		Yes	No	Total
Does money sometimes not last until end of week?	n/a – no money	0	2	**2**
	Yes	41	33	**74**
	No	8	4	**12**
	Don't know yet	6	0	**6**
Total		55	39	94

The detrimental effect of participating in education and training

It is conventionally assumed that young people are disadvantaged if they are unemployed, dependent on benefits and lacking educational qualifications. Chapter Two demonstrated the importance that the Labour government has attached to education and training as the means for young people to escape social exclusion. However, one surprising finding of this research was that participating in these activities appeared to have a detrimental effect on young people's tenancy outcomes.

The link between participation in training and tenancy outcomes is perhaps a little tentative, as it is based only on the sources of the young women's incomes at the time of their first contact with advice workers (whose role is discussed further in the next chapter). This variable was statistically related to tenancy outcomes (p=0.075). Although the relationship was a complex one, it appeared that young women who had no income at this point in time, or who were in receipt of Income Support, were likely to succeed in their tenancies. In contrast, those who were in receipt of a training allowance were particularly likely to fail (Table 3.4).

Table 3.4: Cross table of whether tenancy successful by source of income at first contact with advice workers: women only

| | | Tenancy successful? | | |
		Yes	No	Total
Source of income at first contact with advice workers	Nil income	13	4	**17**
	Jobseeker's Allowance (JSA)	8	6	**14**
	Income Support (IS)	9	1	**10**
	Training allowance	1	5	**6**
	IS and child benefit	3	2	**5**
	Wages	1	2	**3**
	JSA and IS	0	1	**1**
	Other	2	4	**6**
	Not known	15	8	**23**
Total		52	33	85

The success of the young women on nil income at this stage – compared to the failure of both tenants who had no income at the time of the first interview – is a paradox that will be considered in more detail in Chapter Four.

The data presented a clearer picture in relation to GCSEs. Tenancy failure was particularly likely for first interview respondents who had either failed to achieve any of these qualifications or who were still studying for them (p=0.038). The four respondents who were still studying for GCSEs at the time of the first interview were all young women (two of whom were lone parents): all four subsequently failed in their tenancies.

The research suggests, therefore, that seeking to maintain a daytime activity, while also beginning an independent tenancy, may be one responsibility too many for 16- and 17-year-olds.

The impact of residualisation

The finding that young people rehoused into Cruddas Park and Benwell were more likely than others to fall into debt between the interviews was the only indication that difficulties in independent living were increased by living in a particular area. A much more influential factor was young people's opinion of the area that they were living in.

Part of the process of applying as homeless was for respondents to identify their preferred area for rehousing, although staff at the homeless section often advised young people that they were most likely to be offered accommodation in an area where they had lived previously. Respondents' preferences for rehousing were fairly evenly split between the six areas – the only exception was a smaller number wishing to be rehoused in Benwell. The housing department's response to these preferences was positive: over 90% of respondents who moved into self-contained accommodation were rehoused in the area of their choice.

Interview data showed that most respondents were initially happy with both the accommodation that they were allocated and the area that it was in, although a less clear picture emerged after six months of independent living. A total of 87 of the 94 first interview respondents (92.6%) said that they liked the property that they were living in. In the case of the 45 young people interviewed at the second stage, 41 initially liked the accommodation, but this had fallen to 34 (75.6%) by the time of the second interview. Common reasons given for now disliking the accommodation were that it was too small (in four cases) and that there were problems with the state of repair (in two cases).

One surprising finding among the sample as a whole (p=0.009), and young women in particular (p=0.047), was that the type of property that they were rehoused into had an effect on their tenancy outcomes, with those rehoused into low-rise flats being particularly likely to fail. The reasons for this finding were unclear, particularly as potential intervening variables – such as area of rehousing and whether the respondent liked the accommodation at the first interview – were found to have no statistically significant effect. It may be that there are disadvantages to young people in living in blocks of flats, but that these are offset in high-rise blocks by the extra security features added by the local authority (as discussed in the next chapter).

Among the first interview respondents, 81 (86.2%) said that they liked the area they were living in. The most common reason for taking a positive view was that family or friends (or both) lived nearby – 50 respondents (53.2% of interviewees) gave this reason. In addition, 33 (35.1%) liked the area because they had been brought up there, lived there for a long time or knew the area well and 18 (19.1%) commented favourably that the area was quiet or did not have much crime (multiple answers to the question were possible).

It would seem from these responses that the availability of informal support was more important to the sample than a feeling of safety. However, the 10 first interview respondents who did not like the area commented mainly on problems associated with crime – specifically they mentioned violence, gangs of disruptive youths and drug taking. Only two said that they disliked the area because it was too far away from their family and friends. Considering the question of security further, 86 first interview respondents (91.5%) said that they felt safe in their accommodation while eight (8.5%) said that they did not.

There had been a sharp fall in the number of respondents liking the area that they lived in at the second interview: 28 of the 45 (62.2%) now had a positive view, compared to 38 at the time of the first interview. The accessibility of family and friends still dominated the reasons for having positive feelings about the area, with the view that it was a quiet area or there was not much trouble being the only other reasons given. Again, this provided a contrast with reasons for disliking the area, where the experience of social problems dominated (see Table 3.5).

So the increasing number of respondents who disliked the area at the time of the second interview appears to indicate that, for some, concerns over crime and social problems were now outweighing the advantages of having a support network nearby. This view is supported by the finding that, although a large majority of second interview respondents (37 or 82.2%) still felt safe in their accommodation, this figure had fallen (from 42) since the time of the first interview.

As might be expected, reasons for feeling unsafe in accommodation also focused on a fear of crime. Two second interview respondents said that they

Table 3.5: Reasons for disliking area: second interview

Reason	Frequency
Crime problems/fear of crime	6
Rough area	3
Too noisy	3
People drinking in area/too many drunks	2
Too far from family and friends	2
Lots of fighting	2
Burgled	2

felt unsafe because of burglaries in the area, while one gave the reason that they had been burgled and another that there had been a mugging outside the front door. Two felt unsafe because of people they knew (an ex-partner in one case and a friend with keys to the property in another), while in three cases the feeling arose from people unknown to them (gangs of youths, 'undesirable' people in the area and the author of an anonymous letter saying that the property was being watched). Only two respondents felt that the property itself was not secure (multiple answers to the question were possible).

The fear of crime expressed by some second interview respondents seemed realistic when considering that seven (15.6%) had experienced a break-in and three (6.7%) an attempted break-in. However, this variable was not statistically related to whether a respondent felt safe or unsafe in their property, so the respondents who feared crime were not necessarily those who had been victims.

When the nine second interview respondents who had moved from their original accommodation were asked to give one or more reasons for leaving, three mentioned loneliness, three that they disliked the accommodation and two that they had experienced financial difficulties. However, six mentioned at least one factor related to the immediate environment: for example, neighbour problems, a break-in or attempted break-in, harassment and being frightened when in the property alone.

The importance of respondents' feelings about the area they were living in was demonstrated by the finding that those who disliked the area at the first interview were more likely to experience tenancy failure ($p=0.014$). This finding also emerged when considering tenancy outcomes for young women only ($p=0.029$). As being close to friends and family was the most frequently given reason for liking an area, and factors associated with crime and security were the main reasons for disliking it, the implications for housing organisations seem clear. Young people are more likely to have a positive experience of independent living if they are allocated a property that is close to their family and friends and in an area that they perceive to be safe. However, positive feelings about an area can be changed by either the experience of, or a growing fear of, crime and antisocial behaviour.

The role of individual factors

The substantial experience of social problems

While the sample were clearly anxious to avoid areas where they believed that there was a concentration of social problems, another issue raised by the research was the extent to which they were, or had been, involved in activities that might be considered unwise or antisocial.

When first interview respondents were asked to classify themselves in terms of their drinking behaviour, a majority (56 or 59.6%) classified themselves as occasional drinkers, with 19 (20.2%) saying that they were non-drinkers and 10 (10.6%) that they were former drinkers. Only six (6.4%) classified themselves as regular and frequent drinkers and only one as a heavy drinker (two respondents did not answer the question). Although the figures do not make for easy comparisons, this reported level of alcohol consumption does not seem particularly high compared to the estimate of the Social Exclusion Unit (2000a, p 22) that one in twelve 16- and 17-year-olds (8.3%) drink three or more times per week.

There were also similarities with other young people in relation to drug taking: 51 first interview respondents (54.3%) had taken drugs at some point in their lives, which was only slightly higher than the figure of one in two 16-19 year-olds who have tried drugs according to the estimate of the Social Exclusion Unit (2000a, p 22). Similarly, 19 first interview respondents (20.2%) said that they were currently taking drugs – with seven saying that they took them daily – while national figures show that 25.3% of 16 to 29-year-olds in England and Wales, and 21.4% of those in the North East, reported taking an illegal drug in 2000 (ONS, 2003c).

However, a different pattern emerged when respondents were asked how often they smoked, with 71 (75.5%) classifying themselves as daily smokers. This compares with the Social Exclusion Unit's (2000a, p 22) estimate that one in three 16 to 19-year-olds smoke regularly. There was a less than 0.1% risk of error in concluding that 16- and 17-year-olds rehoused as homeless in Newcastle are more likely to smoke than 16 to 19-year-olds nationally.

While smoking is often thought of as unwise and unhealthy rather than antisocial, the difficult relationship that many sample members appeared to experience with people in authority might be regarded as more problematic. Fifty-two first interview respondents (55.3%) said that they had regularly failed to attend school. While figures across an entire school career are not available, the Youth Cohort Study has suggested that 2% of year 11 pupils truant for weeks at a time and 2% for several days at a time – figures that seem extremely low compared to the data provided by this sample (SEU, 1998, p 4). In addition, a significant minority of first interview respondents had been involved in criminal behaviour, with 37 (39.4%) having been in trouble with the police at some point. According to the Home Office (2000, p 38), 23% of 14- to 18-year-old males, and 8% of females of the same age, have been sentenced on three or more occasions. Although not an exact comparison, the percentage of young people in the study who had been in trouble with the police three times or more was 47.8% for males and 12.7% for females.

The offences that had resulted in this contact with the police are shown in Table 3.6.

Six of the young people interviewed at the second stage (13.3%) had been in trouble with the police since the first interview, suggesting that a minority of the sample would experience continuing problems. Being in trouble with the police was clearly an undesirable outcome of independent living, so investigations were undertaken to establish which variables affected the likelihood of such trouble occurring between the first and second interviews.

A predictable finding was that alcohol consumption was influential: those

Table 3.6: Offences of respondents

Offence	Frequency
Burglary/attempted burglary/robbery/theft	15
Shoplifting	12
Assault/violence/violent disorder	11
Criminal damage	8
Stealing cars	5
Drunkenness/drunk and disorderly	3
Drug possession	2
'Petty' crimes	2
Wounding with intent	2
Other	10

young people who classified themselves as former drinkers, or as regular and frequent drinkers, were particularly likely to have had police contact in the early months of their tenancy, with occasional drinkers and non-drinkers more likely to have avoided trouble (p=0.005). There was also evidence to suggest that material hardship had an effect: respondents who reported their money situation to be "quite poor" or "very poor" at the first interview were particularly likely to subsequently be in trouble with the police (p=0.067). Finally, respondents' feelings about independent living seemed to be a relevant factor, with those who initially felt poorly prepared for living away from home or care being particularly likely to have been in trouble with the police between the interviews (p=0.03).

So a variety of factors affected the likelihood that a respondent would be in trouble with the police in the early months of their tenancy. To examine further the sample's experience of social problems, analysis was undertaken of the relationships between the following first interview variables:

- whether attended school regularly;
- whether achieved any GCSEs;
- whether currently taking drugs;
- whether been in trouble with the police.

Statistically significant relationships were found between almost all of these variables – the only two that appeared to be independent of each other were whether a respondent had achieved any GCSEs and whether they had been in trouble with the police. In some cases the evidence of these relationships confirmed national research findings: for example, research that has shown that the likelihood of committing crime is increased by absence from school (SEU, 2002, p 44) and taking drugs (SEU, 2002, p 62).

The impact of multiple social problems was investigated by devising an index showing the number of problems that young people had experienced, or were experiencing, from these variables. The 'scores' of the first interview respondents on this index are shown in Table 3.7.

Respondents who had high scores on this index were particularly likely to

Table 3.7: Number of social problems experienced by respondents

Number of problems	Frequency	%
4	10	11.6
3	19	22.1
2	22	25.6
1	14	16.3
0	21	24.4
Total	86	100.0

Note: In eight cases, not all of the information was available to calculate the score.

experience difficulties in independent living. They were more likely than other respondents to be in debt at the time of the first interview (p=0.042) and more likely to fail in their tenancies (p=0.069). These findings, while unsurprising, indicated that there was a group of young people in particular need of support services.

Changing perceptions of independent living

Although the extent to which young people had been involved in social problems influenced their experience of independent living, another factor that could be seen as an individual failing – feeling overconfident – appeared to have a more substantial effect. This was particularly well illustrated by the answers to questions about respondents' perceptions of independent living. First interview responses were measured against answers at the second interview, and compared to tenancy outcomes, in an attempt to evaluate the realism and maturity with which the sample had approached living in their own property.

At a practical level, first interview respondents were asked about a range of domestic abilities. Fifty-eight (61.7%) said that they could cook proper meals and 30 (31.9%) that they knew how to cook a few things. The responses to other questions asking whether they were able to undertake other selected household tasks are shown in Table 3.8.

Table 3.8: Number of respondents able to undertake household tasks

Question	Yes	No
Know how to wash clothes?	83 (88.3%)	11 (11.7%)
Know how to iron clothes?	90 (95.7%)	4 (4.3%)
Know how to keep place clean?	92 (97.9%)	2 (2.1%)
Know how to use a heating system?	80 (85.1%)	14 (14.9%)
Know how to turn gas and electric on and off?	82 (87.2%)	12 (12.8%)
Know how to act if there is a gas leak?[a]	54 (57.4%)	38 (40.4%)
Know how to act if there is a water leak?	60 (63.8%)	34 (36.2%)

Note: [a] In two cases (2.1%) this question was not applicable, because there was no gas.

The responses to these questions were combined into an index of domestic abilities, which showed that 79 of 92 respondents (85.9%) felt that they had five or more of the seven skills[2]. There was a similar level of confidence displayed in response to a question asking how well prepared first interview respondents felt for leaving home or care: 78 (83%) said that they felt completely ready or more or less ready, with only 16 (17%) saying that they felt not quite ready or not ready at all.

Similarly, 71 first interview respondents (75.5%) felt that they had had enough advice about independent living while only 20 (21.3%) felt that they had not, with three (3.2%) unable to give an answer. The sample was most likely to feel inadequately advised over financial matters such as paying bills, budgeting, claiming benefits or finding other sources of financial assistance.

The pattern of widespread confidence, tempered only by some concerns about managing financially, was reproduced when respondents were asked whether they expected to experience any problems in living independently. A majority felt that they would not have any problems, but 22 of the 28 who expected difficulties thought that these would arise over money matters. Only nine first interview respondents (9.6%) had regrets about leaving their family home or care: of these, two wanted to be back with their family and two wished they could have waited to be in a better financial position before leaving.

However, despite their generally positive views, 70 first interview respondents (74.5%) could identify at least one disadvantage of independent living. Financial problems were again the most commonly identified difficulty, but a number of respondents also mentioned getting lonely or being alone and having to do household tasks such as tidying up, cooking and washing.

Only one first interview respondent was unable to identify any advantage of living in their own accommodation. A total of 79 (84.0%) cited independence as an advantage, expressing this in terms of being able to do what they wanted, making their own decisions, having freedom or not being told what to do. Other advantages commonly identified were having the house to themselves or having their own space (mentioned by 11 respondents), and privacy (mentioned by seven).

The second interview showed the extent to which feelings about independent living had changed in the first few months of the tenancy. It has already been noted that smaller numbers said at the second interview that they liked the area, that they liked the property they were living in or that they felt safe within it. There was a similar reduction in confidence about the ability to live independently. Only 11 of the 45 second interview respondents (24.4%) said that they had been completely ready for leaving home or care, compared to 22 (48.9%) who had said this at the time of the first interview. The number of young people who said that they had been not quite ready, or not ready at all, had risen from nine (20%) to 19 (42.2%). Looking back, 26 respondents (57.8%) felt that they had had enough advice about independent living, compared to 34 (75.6%) who had said this at the time of the first interview. Of the 19 who now felt that they had been inadequately advised, 16 identified money, budgeting or financial issues as the matters on which they had lacked information: no other subject was raised by more than one respondent.

A range of other responses also suggested that concerns over financial issues had increased since the time of the first interview. For example, 32 second interview respondents identified a financial factor as a disadvantage of independent living compared to 17 who had identified similar disadvantages at the first interview. Of the 12 respondents who now had regrets about obtaining their own tenancy (compared to four at the first interview), financial factors and missing family were again the most common reasons for these regrets. A new question asked at the second interview revealed that 22 respondents (48.9%) felt that not enough support was provided to young people moving into independent housing − financial assistance and benefits advice dominated the list of areas where respondents thought that extra support should be provided. In addition, 16 second interview respondents (35.6%) said that they had experienced unforeseen difficulties while living in their own property. These difficulties related to money or debt in 12 cases, while four respondents mentioned burglary and two harassment by local youths (multiple responses could be given).

So financial difficulties appeared to be the most important reason for falling confidence among second interview respondents, although crime and antisocial behaviour also seemed to play a part. While material hardship may have had a limited impact on the outcome of tenancies, it appeared to substantially affect young people's feeling about their own property.

Despite the less positive view of second interview respondents, they were still able to identify advantages to living in their own property: 40 thought independence or being their own boss was an advantage, while 11 said privacy or having their own space was. In addition, there was still a majority of second interview respondents who gave positive answers to the following questions:

- Do you like the actual accommodation you currently have?
- Do you generally like the area in which you live?
- Do you generally feel safe in your accommodation?
- Looking back, when I spoke to you the last time, how ready do you think you were for having your own tenancy?
- Looking back, do you feel that you had enough advice about living in independent accommodation?

In order to establish a broader picture of changes to respondents' feelings, an index was compiled, consisting of answers to these questions and their first interview equivalents. For each question, a respondent was awarded a score of +1 if they felt more positively at the second interview (for example, if they disliked the property at the time of the first interview but liked it at the second), 0 if they felt the same and –1 if they gave a less positive response. A respondent's total was then calculated by adding the scores across the variables.

The four respondents who had answered "don't know" to one of the questions were not given an index score. Of the other 41 second interview respondents, 30 (73.1%) were less positive in their overall feelings about independent living than they had been at the time of the first interview, six (14.6%) had unchanged feelings and only five (12.2%) now felt more positive.

The dangers of overconfidence

The changes to feelings about independent living by the time of the second interview suggested that the sample had been unduly optimistic when they first moved into their properties. Further investigations were undertaken to establish whether there were factors that increased the likelihood that a respondent would experience a reduction in confidence after six months of independent living. The relationship between changes to feelings and some variables was a complex one, but a number of clear findings emerged.

Those young people who scored three or four on the index of social problems were particularly likely to feel less positive at the second interview, which further emphasises the disadvantage experienced by this group. Respondents who had children at the time of the second interview were more likely to have feelings that were unchanged or more positive – indeed all five of those who now felt more positive were mothers ($p=0.033$). This finding remained significant ($p=0.053$) when considering young women only. The protection against deteriorating feelings that the lone parents appeared to enjoy was one of a number of advantages that they had over the remainder of the sample, as will be shown later in this chapter.

There were also a number of indications that respondents who were more realistic about their situation at the first interview were less likely to be feeling disappointed with the experience of independent living by the time of the second. There was a statistically significant relationship between the score on the index of changes to feelings and a respondent's assessment of their own cooking ability at the first interview ($p=0.073$), with none of the respondents who admitted to not being able to cook subsequently experiencing less positive feelings. In addition, respondents who said that their accommodation was inadequately furnished at the first interview were less likely to experience deteriorating feelings ($p=0.029$), as were those who initially said that they did not have many friends ($p=0.048$). While believing that your accommodation is inadequately furnished, feeling unable to cook and thinking that you do not have many friends may seem an odd combination of factors to be linked to stable feelings about independent living, they all suggest that a realistic initial view can protect against later disappointment.

Findings about a respondent's assessment of their own health followed the opposite pattern, with those respondents who gave a positive assessment at the first interview being less vulnerable to deteriorating feelings about independent living by the second ($p=0.057$). However, discriminant analysis showed this to be the first interview variable that had the least effect on the changes to a respondent's feelings: the number of problems had the greatest effect, followed by the three variables that suggested that initial negative (or realistic) feelings could help to prevent disappointment at a later stage.

The evidence that many sample members had unrealistically high expectations of independent living might not be of major concern to landlords unless there were also indications that these expectations were adversely affecting the outcome of tenancies. It has already been noted that those respondents who were still waiting for benefit payments at the first interview were particularly likely to conduct successful tenancies, suggesting that an initial awareness of difficulties can have a beneficial effect in the longer term. Similarly, two variables suggested that overconfidence had a detrimental effect. Respondents who did not express any regrets about moving into their own tenancy at the first interview were particularly likely to fail ($p=0.077$). In addition, the score on the index of domestic abilities was shown to have a statistically significant impact on tenancy outcomes ($p=0.037$). As might be expected, respondents who felt that their domestic skills were very limited were particularly likely to fail, but so were those who said that they had all seven of the abilities included in the index (see Table 3.9).

When limiting the analysis of variables affecting the outcome of tenancies to young women only, it appeared that they were the group who were particularly likely to fail if they were overconfident, and so would benefit most from a more cautious/realistic approach. Three of the relationships between variables that have been noted for the sample as a whole also applied when considering young women only: they were more likely to succeed in their tenancies if, at the first interview, they did not know whether their money would last until the end of the week ($p=0.073$), they expressed regrets about moving into their own tenancy ($p=0.029$) and they rated their domestic abilities as being neither very high nor very low ($p=0.025$).

So, when considering the view that young people's difficulties in independent living are caused by their inexperience or immaturity, the data offered some evidence to suggest that unrealistically high expectations were linked to tenancy failure, particularly for young women. This was one of a number of areas where evidence of gender differences emerged from the research.

Table 3.9: Cross table of whether tenancy successful by score on index of domestic abilities

		Tenancy successful?		
		Yes	No	Total
Domestic abilities	Can perform all 7 functions	17	18	**35**
	Can perform 6 functions	17	4	**21**
	Can perform 5 functions	15	8	**23**
	Can perform 4 functions	4	3	**7**
	Can perform 3 functions	0	3	**3**
	Can perform 2 functions	1	2	**3**
Total		54	38	92

Differences between different groups of young people

Gender differences

In making comparisons between the young men and the young women in the sample, it is acknowledged that one reason for differences might be that some of the young women had children living with them. In the analysis that follows, gender differences remained statistically significant after eliminating young women with children, unless otherwise stated.

The most striking difference to emerge from the data was the greater likelihood of young men having experienced high numbers of social problems ($p<0.001$). Indeed, the majority of the young men had experienced three or four of the problems included in the social problem index (see Table 3.10).

Considering the problems individually, men in the sample were less likely to have obtained any GCSEs or to have attended school regularly, but these differences were not statistically significant. However, there was a significant difference in drug taking ($p<0.001$) with a majority of young men taking drugs at the time of the first interview, compared to only six of the 69 young women. Similarly, 20 of the 23 men had tried drugs at some time in their life, compared to 31 of the 69 women ($p=0.001$). Another striking finding was the greater likelihood of the young men having been in trouble with the police ($p<0.001$) (see Table 3.11).

There were also gender differences in the feelings that young people had about independent living. All 23 of the men identified independence as an advantage of having their own accommodation, compared to 56 of the 71

Table 3.10: Cross table of number of problems by gender

		Gender		
		Male	Female	Total
Number of problems	4	8	2	10
	3	7	12	19
	2	3	19	22
	1	3	11	14
	0	1	20	21
Total		22	64	86

Table 3.11: Cross table of gender by whether been in trouble with the police

		Gender		
		Male	Female	Total
Been in trouble with the police?	Yes	19	18	37
	No	4	52	56
Total		23	70	93

women (*p*=0.018). Despite the great value that they placed on their independence, the young men were also less confident about living in their own property – they were more likely to say at the first interview that they expected problems in independent living (*p*=0.006). However, unlike the young women, there was no indication that the young men who felt less confident were more likely to succeed in their tenancies. Indeed, the opposite pattern appeared to apply, with those young men who said, at the first interview, that they had not been given enough advice about independent living being particularly likely to fail (*p*=0.086). The implications of these gender differences for support services will be discussed in the next two chapters.

The young men's less positive expectations did not appear to arise from concerns over their skills in household tasks: the index of domestic abilities showed no statistically significant gender differences. Additional analysis suggested that there was only one task included in the index where a significant difference existed: all 71 of the young women said that they knew how to iron clothes, compared to 19 of the 23 young men (*p*=0.003).

The young men were more likely to experience material disadvantage. Their average weekly income was £36.50 at the time of the first interview, compared to a figure of £44 for the young women who did not have children. The young men were less likely to rate their health as "very good" or "good" (*p*=0.01). They were less likely to say that they ate a healthy diet (*p*=0.033), although this difference ceased to be statistically significant when eliminating both young women with children and those who were pregnant from the analysis.

Given the range of disadvantages experienced by the young men, it is perhaps unsurprising that they were less likely to be successful in their tenancies (*p*=0.023) (see Table 3.12).

Young men's tenancy outcomes were affected by their relationship with agencies, the number of social problems that they had experienced and whether they had stayed in local authority temporary accommodation, all of which are discussed further in later sections.

Favourable experiences of lone parents

The relatively positive position of female members of the sample was emphasised by the favourable experience of independent living that lone parents appeared to enjoy. The number of young women who had children living with them at the time of the first interview was 12. This number had increased substantially,

Table 3.12: Cross table of whether tenancy successful by gender

		Tenancy successful?		
		Yes	No	Total
Gender	Male	14	24	**38**
	Female	64	43	**107**
Total		78	67	145

to 20, by the time of the second interview. Where analysis later in this chapter suggests a statistically significant difference between respondents who had children and those who did not, this difference remained significant when considering young women only, unless otherwise stated.

The protection that having children appeared to offer against deteriorating feelings about independent living has already been identified. An examination of first interview data provided no evidence to suggest that this was due to lone parents feeling less positive initially. The numbers were too small to establish statistically significant differences with the remainder of the sample, but among the respondents who had children at the time of the first interview:

- all liked the accommodation that they were living in;
- all liked the area that they were living in; and
- all felt safe in their accommodation.

However, these positive feelings were tempered with realism, as was demonstrated by the responses to the first interview question asking whether a young person felt that they had had enough advice about living independently. Respondents with children were less likely to answer "no" than the remainder of the sample, but more likely to answer "don't know" ($p=0.001$).

Young lone parents also seemed to have avoided some of the social problems that were so prevalent among the remainder of the sample. None of the first or second interview respondents with children were taking drugs and the first interview data showed that the lone parents were less likely than other respondents to have ever tried them ($p=0.036$). Although this relationship ceased to be statistically significant when considering young women only, one finding that was unambiguous was that respondents with children were less likely to have been in trouble with the police ($p=0.001$, or $p=0.01$ when considering young women only).

So lone parents felt positively about independent living at the first interview, were less likely than other sample members to lose their positive feelings by the time of the second interview and were also less likely to have been in trouble with the police. The reasons for this relatively favourable picture can only be a matter for speculation. However, the findings suggest that the government's focus on the problems of lone parents living independently is inappropriate. Although the young men were a minority of the sample, they seemed to be a group who would be a more appropriate focus for policy concern.

The role of informal support

As might be expected with a sample of 16- and 17-year-olds, the most common reason for their initial homelessness was a breakdown in family relationships. The records of the homeless section showed that, in 111 of the 145 cases (76.6%), the reason for the young person applying as homeless was that one or both parents were unable to keep them.

More respondents stayed temporarily with friends or relatives while awaiting rehousing (73 or 50.4%) than stayed in the family home (55 or 37.9%), suggesting that the breakdown in relationship with parents often resulted in the young person needing to leave immediately. Only 22 respondents (15.2%) stayed in the local authority's temporary accommodation at Hill Court or New Bridge Street.

The positive role of most families

Despite the sample being unable to live in the family home, they received substantial support from their parents and from other informal sources. It has already been noted that the reason respondents gave most frequently for liking the area they were living in was that it was close to family, friends or both.

The extent of informal support available was further illustrated by 82 of the 94 first interview respondents (87.2%) saying that they had been offered advice about living independently. The most common sources of advice were parents or relatives (in 53 cases) and friends (in 39 cases, multiple answers to the question were possible). This advice was almost universally felt to have been very helpful or quite helpful.

In addition, 83 first interview respondents (88.3%) said that they had quite a few friends and 71 (75.5%) that their family and friends were a good help to them. The frequency with which respondents saw their parents is shown in Figure 3.2.

Figure 3.2: How often respondents saw their parents: first interview

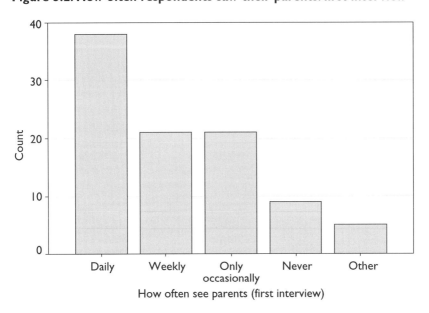

The picture of positive informal relationships was reinforced by 64 respondents (68.1%) saying that they got on well with their family, while 20 (21.3%) said that they did not. The remaining 10 (10.6%) qualified their answer in some way: for example, two said that they got on well if they did what they were told.

The research offered no evidence to suggest that young people from lone-parent families received less informal support than others. Leaving aside cases where a young person had not been living in the family home prior to their homelessness, it was possible – based on the information provided by the homeless section – to identify whether a respondent had been living with one parent or both in 111 cases. The analysis of these 111 cases suggested that there was no statistically significant relationship between family structure and how often a respondent saw their parents, how well they got on with their family and whether they considered their family and friends to be a good help.

There were also no statistically significant differences between young men and young women – or between respondents with and without children – when considering any of the 'family' variables. However, one group that was disadvantaged in relation to informal support was care leavers, who were particularly likely to say that their family and friends were not a good help to them ($p=0.096$).

The sample's appreciation of informal support appeared to increase with the amount of time spent living independently. By the time of the second interview, 41 respondents said that their family and friends were a good help to them, compared to 35 who had said this at the first interview. A majority of second interview respondents were in daily contact with their parents: 26 (or 57.8%), compared to 19 at the time of the first interview. Asked how their relationship with their parents had changed since the first interview, 25 respondents (55.6%) said that it had improved, 16 (35.6%) that it had stayed the same and only four (8.9%) that it had got worse.

The importance of positive family relationships was demonstrated by difficulties experienced by the minority of the sample whose relationships were problematic. First interview respondents who said that they did not get on well with their family were particularly likely to subsequently be in trouble with the police ($p=0.052$).

However, more striking was the disadvantage experienced by the four second interview respondents who said that their relationship with their parents had deteriorated since the time of the first interview. One of these respondents was living back with her mother; the other three all thought that their accommodation was inadequately furnished ($p=0.001$, when compared to other second interview respondents). Three of the four disliked the accommodation they were living in ($p=0.043$) and all four had immediate plans to move ($p=0.005$). These four young people were also more likely than other respondents to be taking drugs at the time of the second interview ($p=0.001$) and to feel, in retrospect, that they had not been ready for living away from home or care ($p=0.094$).

The second interview findings raise the question of whether the four respondents had suffered similar types of disadvantage at the time of the first interview or whether, in comparison to other second interview respondents, their situation had deteriorated with time. The relationship with parents was likely to have been a poor one from the start: three of the four had said at the first interview that they did not get on well with their family. In addition, when asked how often they saw their parents, four responses had been daily, weekly, only occasionally and never.

However, analysis of other first interview variables suggested that the disadvantage experienced by this group had not been so severe at the start of the tenancy. When interviewed the first time, the four respondents had been no more likely than others to say that they disliked their accommodation, that it was inadequately furnished or that they felt badly prepared for leaving home or care. In contrast, there were several strands of evidence to suggest that a deteriorating relationship with parents was likely to be accompanied by an increase in other difficulties. Comparing the second interview responses with the first interview data for this group showed that two who used to like their accommodation now did not, two who previously thought that their accommodation was adequately furnished now did not and three gave a less positive answer as to how ready they had been for living away from home or care.

There was, however, one form of disadvantage that had existed at the time of the first interview for respondents whose relationship with their parents subsequently deteriorated. They had been more likely than other respondents to have a high score on the index of social problems ($p=0.008$) and, in particular, more likely to be taking drugs ($p=0.006$) (see Table 3.13).

So it is perhaps most helpful to think of family relationships – and particularly the manner in which they develop during a tenancy – as an indicator of the difficulties that a young person is likely to experience in independent living. However, returning to the key concern for housing managers, none of the 'family' variables had a statistically significant bearing on the outcome of tenancies. Instead, such an effect was found when considering variables that were broader indicators of social isolation.

Table 3.13: Cross table of how relationship with parents changed by whether take drugs at present: first interview

		How relationship with parents changed			
		Improved	Stayed the same	Got worse	Total
Taking drugs at	Yes	2	1	3	**6**
first interview?	No	23	14	1	**38**
Total		25	15	4	44

The disadvantage of the most isolated young people

It might be assumed that the 22 young people who stayed in the local authority's temporary accommodation were the most socially isolated group in the sample, as they could not stay temporarily with friends, parents or other relatives. A slightly surprising finding, therefore, was that there were no statistically significant differences between this group and the rest of the sample when considering the variables linked to family relationships. However, they were less likely than other respondents to say at the first interview that they had quite a few friends ($p=0.007$), suggesting that they faced a particularly high risk of isolation for their peer group.

It has already been shown that the young people who stayed in local authority temporary accommodation were particularly likely to have debts at the time of the first interview. The first interview data showed that they were also more likely than other respondents to:

- dislike the area that they were living in ($p=0.053$);
- feel that they had been inadequately advised about independent living ($p=0.013$);
- have experienced high numbers of social problems ($p=0.007$);
- have tried drugs at some time in their life ($p=0.057$);
- be currently taking drugs ($p=0.024$); and
- have been in trouble with the police ($p=0.031$).

It was noted earlier that the last four of these factors were also particularly likely to affect male respondents. Indeed, the study of the temporary accommodation group was complicated by the predominance of young men: 12 of the 38 male members of the sample had stayed there, compared to only 10 of the 107 young women ($p=0.002$). Discriminant analysis showed that being male had a greater effect than staying in local authority temporary accommodation on the likelihood of experiencing a high number of social problems, taking drugs at the time of the first interview or in the past, and having been in trouble with the police.

There was clearly a close relationship between being male, staying in local authority temporary accommodation, experiencing high numbers of social problems and tenancy failure. As with young men and respondents with high scores on the social problem index, the temporary accommodation group were particularly likely to fail in their tenancies ($p=0.001$) (see Table 3.14).

Young men were particularly likely to fail if they had stayed in local authority temporary accommodation ($p=0.027$) and those who had stayed in such accommodation were particularly likely to fail if they were male ($p=0.056$). Indeed, the tenancy failure of 11 of the 12 young men who had stayed in temporary accommodation was one of the most striking findings of this research.

Unlike the young men – who were more likely to fail in their tenancies if they had experienced all four of the problems on the index ($p=0.024$) – there

Table 3.14: Cross table of whether tenancy successful by whether stayed temporarily in local authority temporary accommodation

		Tenancy successful?		
		Yes	**No**	**Total**
Stayed temporarily in local authority	Yes	6	16	22
temporary accommodation?	No	72	51	123
Total		78	67	145

was no relationship between the number of social problems and tenancy outcomes when considering the temporary accommodation group. Instead, factors that increased their risk of tenancy failure were:

- not feeling completely ready for living away from home or care at the time of the first interview ($p=0.087$);
- living with only one parent prior to applying to the local authority as homeless ($p=0.082$: this was the only group where family structure appeared to have an impact on tenancy outcomes); and
- saying at the first interview that they had not received enough advice about independent living ($p=0.021$).

As young men were also more likely to fail if they felt that they had not been given enough advice about living independently, these findings further illustrate the extent of the links between the two groups.

The essential role of friends

Although variables concerning relationships with families did not have an impact on tenancy outcomes – except in the case of the temporary accommodation group, as noted earlier – this was not the case when considering respondents' relationships with their friends. It was noted earlier that the small minority of respondents who felt that they did not have many friends at the time of the first interview were less vulnerable to a subsequent deterioration in feelings about independent living. However, they were also more likely to fail in their tenancies ($p=0.047$), suggesting that the overall effect was a negative one.

There was also evidence to suggest that it was not just having friends and social contacts, but also the nature of the relationships with them, that affected the outcome of tenancies. A huge majority of first interview respondents – 91 of the 94 (96.8%) – said that they had control over who visited them, when they visited and when they left. However, the three respondents who did not feel that they had this control – all of them young women – subsequently failed in their tenancies ($p=0.068$).

One surprising finding of the research was that, although current drug taking was not linked to the outcome of tenancies, there was a greater likelihood of

Table 3.15: Cross table of whether tenancy successful by whether have ever tried drugs

		Tenancy successful?		
		Yes	**No**	**Total**
Ever tried drugs?	Yes	24	27	**51**
	No	29	12	**41**
	Don't know/not stated	2	0	**2**
Total		55	39	94

success among first interview respondents if they had never taken drugs, as is shown by Table 3.15.

One possible explanation for this finding was that respondents who had never tried drugs were less likely to have a peer group who had been involved in this activity and so were less likely to have faced pressure to become involved themselves. Considering the subgroups of the sample, it was young men ($p=0.047$) and young people who had stayed in local authority temporary accommodation ($p=0.077$) where there was a statistically significant relationship between tenancy outcomes and the 'ever tried drugs' variable, which again illustrates the influence of social problems over the experience of these two groups.

Relative importance of factors affecting tenancy outcomes

As the most important aim of this research was to identify the factors that affected success and failure in tenancies, the variables that had been shown to have a statistically significant effect on tenancy outcomes were subject to discriminant analysis. The variables included some not discussed in this chapter, mainly those concerning respondents' relationships with agencies, which are considered further in Chapter Four. All the interview variables subjected to the analysis were taken from the first interview.

For the sample as a whole, the four variables that had the greatest effect over tenancy outcomes were whether a respondent had ever tried drugs, whether they had quite a few friends, whether they had control over their visitors and whether they had stayed in local authority temporary accommodation. This finding clearly illustrates the critical importance of a supportive peer group.

Fifth in the list of most influential variables was a respondent's gender, highlighting again the level of disadvantage experienced by young men. When considering male respondents separately, three variables that had a high level of influence were whether they had stayed in local authority temporary accommodation, whether they had ever tried drugs and whether they felt that they had had enough advice about independent living. Lacking either confidence or a supportive peer group appeared to have a particularly detrimental effect on young men.

The most influential variable for young women was whether they had control over their visitors, which again emphasises the importance of peer group influence. However, there were three highly ranked variables – whether their money lasted until the end of the week, whether they had any regrets about moving into their own tenancy and their score on the index of domestic abilities – which suggested that either initial difficulties, or a cautious approach, could act as protection against overconfidence about independent living. Difficulties caused by a lack of confidence on the part of young men, and overconfidence on the part of young women, suggest very different support needs for these two groups – a point that is returned to in later chapters.

Summary

The key trends to emerge from the data can be summarised as follows:

- The sample were less likely than other young people to have qualifications and to be involved in work, education or training.
- They tended to have low incomes and to find that their money did not last until the end of the week.
- Financial difficulties reduced the likelihood that respondents would take a positive view of their own health.
- A substantial number of the sample were in debt shortly after moving into their own property; this had become a majority after six months of independent living.
- Initial debt was linked to spending on drugs, cigarettes and alcohol.
- Living in a disadvantaged area and receiving inadequate advice about independent living were factors that were linked to debt over a longer time period.
- There were surprisingly few long-term effects of material hardship, although respondents who had no income at the first interview were more likely to fail in their tenancy and those who rated their money situation poorly were more likely to subsequently be in trouble with the police.
- Young women who were participating in education or training were particularly likely to fail in their tenancy.
- Most respondents were rehoused into the area of their choice and liked the area they were living in, largely due to the proximity of family and friends.
- Where respondents disliked the area, it was usually due to the fear of crime.
- Young people who disliked the area that they were living in – particularly the young women – were more likely to fail in their tenancies.
- Young women formed a large majority of the sample, reflecting the higher numbers applying to Newcastle City Council as homeless. The young men were particularly likely to experience a number of disadvantages.
- Lone parents appeared to have a relatively favourable experience of independent living.
- The sample seemed more likely than other young people to smoke, to have truanted from school, to have achieved no GCSEs and to have been in trouble with the police.

- There was a high level of overlap between being male, staying in local authority temporary accommodation and having experienced high numbers of social problems. All of these factors were linked to tenancy failure.
- Many young respondents felt less positively after six months of independent living; this appeared to be particularly likely among those who had initially adopted a very optimistic view.
- Fear of crime and financial hardship had a major influence on declining confidence about independent living.
- Initial overconfidence appeared to be linked to tenancy failure among the young women.
- However, young men were more likely to fail if they felt inadequately advised about independent living, suggesting that lack of confidence was detrimental to them.
- Most respondents reported positive relationships with family and friends.
- The only indications that there were varying levels of informal support available to different groups of young people were that those who had stayed in local authority temporary accommodation were particularly likely to feel that they lacked friends and care leavers were less likely to say that their family and friends were a good help to them.
- The small number of respondents who found that their relationship with their parents had deteriorated after six months in their tenancy were likely to experience a variety of other disadvantages.
- Taking drugs, and having experienced high numbers of social problems, appeared to be the best predictors that a relationship with parents would deteriorate.
- Respondents who felt that they lacked friends were more likely to fail in their tenancies.
- Never having tried drugs – which may be a reflection of the nature of the relationship that a young person had with their peer group – appeared to offer the best protection against tenancy failure.

The implications of these findings will be discussed in later chapters. The next chapter considers the services that have been developed for young people living independently in Newcastle and the impact that they have had on the needs discussed earlier.

Notes

[1] This figure excludes the small number of sample members who were still studying for GCSEs.

[2] The two respondents not given a score on the index were those who did not have gas in the property.

FOUR

The local authority dilemma and the impact of services

Local authority responses to homelessness

The support services received by the sample need to be studied in the context of the response of Newcastle City Council to homelessness, because the first contact that the authority had with most of the young people occurred when they made their homelessness application. This chapter examines the services that were provided from the time of this application to the point where a young person had been living independently for six months.

Newcastle, like many other local authorities, currently provides a range of services to meet the needs of homeless people. This response is in contrast to an initial reluctance by some authorities to meet the obligations placed on them by central government with regard to homelessness. The first major piece of legislation in this area was the 1948 National Assistance Act, which was eventually followed by the 1977 Housing (Homeless Persons) Act and then further legislation, as discussed in Chapter One. In each case, the legislation consisted of central government introducing or amending statutory duties for local authorities. Historically, some authorities resented these obligations, which they saw as providing opportunities for undeserving homeless applicants to 'jump the queue' at the expense of deserving waiting list applicants (see, for example, Richards, 1992, p 130). As a result, authorities often sought to meet their obligations in a minimalist manner – for example, by offering very poor temporary accommodation to homeless households (Watchman and Robson, 1989, pp 38-9; Lund, 1996, p 85).

Two factors appear to have led to a more generous approach being adopted in more recent years. The first was a change to the view that homeless people were undeserving. Somerville (1999, pp 30-1) argues that this was a long-term historic phenomenon, which was influenced by developments such as the eviction of many families from private rented accommodation after the 1957 Rent Act, the displacement of households from properties that were subject to local authority slum clearance programmes, the showing of the documentary *Cathy Come Home* in 1966 and an increasing emphasis in social policy on achieving improvements to the welfare of homeless families.

The second factor was a change in the nature of local authorities, which became more political in the late 1970s and early 1980s. Reasons for this change included the reorganisation of local government in 1974 and the introduction of payments to councillors in 1974-75. These developments led to the major parties contesting more seats (Young and Davies, 1990, p 18) and an increase in the number of full-time councillors (Byrne, 2000, p 534). Even greater impetus towards the politicisation of local government was provided by changes to local political parties in the early 1980s, as the Conservatives adopted the monetarist policies of Mrs Thatcher and middle-class Labour Party activists demanded a more radical socialist programme than Labour had offered at the 1979 general election (Byrne, 2000, pp 540-1).

The politicisation of local government led to clashes between the Conservative central government and Labour-led local authorities. The Conservatives regarded local authorities as key targets for cuts in public expenditure and adopted a confrontational approach to seek to bring about these cuts (Stoker, 1991, pp 12-13). In their first term of office (1979-83), they spoke of "overspending" by local authorities and "value for money", while developing a number of financial mechanisms to seek to control local expenditure (Stoker, 1991, pp 161-5). In their second term, they introduced a system of rate capping, whereby the Secretary of State for the Environment could limit the rates charged by named authorities (and so control their spending). The first list of 18 authorities to be rate capped included 16 controlled by the Labour Party (Stoker, 1991, p 170).

This attempt at greater financial control was vigorously opposed by Labour-controlled authorities, who were seeking to expand the range of services that they provided:

> ... the Conservatives increasingly faced sustained ideological opposition from a range of radical Labour councils, committed not just to protecting existing local government provision but determined to develop new policy responses to social and economic ills in direct challenge to the approach of the Conservatives. (Stoker, 1991, p 162)

Labour-led authorities argued that the state had failed to provide adequate remedies to the problems of poverty and deprivation, and launched their own antipoverty strategies (Alcock, 1994, pp 137-8). Balloch and Jones (1990, pp 40-54) suggest that these strategies could be divided into four key areas: income maintenance and support (for example, insulating property to combat fuel poverty), decentralisation to increase access to local services, economic development (measures to tackle local unemployment) and welfare rights work. Welfare rights was a key element of the services to meet the needs of young people living independently in Newcastle during this period, as will be shown later in this chapter.

The commitment of many local authorities to maintain and develop services for disadvantaged groups in the face of central government hostility was reflected in more generous treatment for homeless households and the provision of services beyond those required by the law. Somerville (1999, p 35) argues that, by the end of the 1980s, local authority opposition to the homelessness legislation had all but disappeared. Butler et al (1994, p 19) showed that many authorities were providing services to homeless people beyond those required by law: for example, 56% provided visiting support after rehousing.

This more generous approach extended to young people: it was noted in Chapter One that the number of authorities accepting 16- and 17-year-olds as being in priority need on the grounds of their age increased substantially between the study of Venn (1985) and that of Kay (1994). Gilroy (1993) noted that a wide range of services was being developed for young people among a sample of 89 local authorities. Many of the initiatives were concerned simply with the provision of accommodation: 26 authorities had provided purpose-built units for young people, 21 had converted property into shared units and 48 were letting family-sized units to sharers (Gilroy, 1993, p 12). Similarly, Kay's (1994, pp 19-21) study found that almost half the local authorities surveyed had designated stock for 16- and 17-year-olds and that 28% had plans to develop accommodation for this age group.

Gilroy also found evidence of services designed to overcome two of the types of difficulty in independent living that were discussed in Chapter One. Firstly, and consistent with the broader local authority agenda of tackling poverty and deprivation, there were initiatives to meet material needs. Furnished units for young people had been provided by 37 authorities (Gilroy, 1993, p 12), eight operated their own furniture store and nine provided debt counsellors (Gilroy, 1993, p 17). Secondly, there were services that might be seen as tackling young people's inexperience. Intensively managed units were provided by 31 authorities (Gilroy, 1993, p 12) and five employed support workers for young people (Gilroy, 1993, p 17).

Gilroy's study demonstrated the extent of the commitment of many local authorities to providing services to young people living independently. However, such services may have become more difficult to develop as a result of new methods of controlling the work of local authorities, beyond simple financial restrictions, that were introduced under the Conservatives and have since been developed further by the Labour governments.

The centre imposes tighter controls

Walker (2000, pp 286-7) notes that the management of social housing has been affected in recent years by "managerialisation" – the Conservative governments imposed a performance-driven model of housing management on local authorities. A key mechanism for introducing the more managerial approach was compulsory competitive tendering. The 1988 Local Government Act gave the government powers to specify local authority services that could only be carried out by their own workforce if the work was won in competition (AMA, 1994). Local authority housing management services were added to the list of services that other organisations were to be invited to tender for in 1993 (Shaw et al, 1996, p 10).

Byrne (2000, p 542) notes that confrontation between central and local government was defused by the election of the Labour government in 1997. However, although not as hostile to local authorities as its predecessors, New Labour has enthusiastically endorsed the idea of measuring the work of the public sector, albeit through performance targets rather than direct competition with other organisations. Instead of being forced to put services out to tender, councils are now required to demonstrate that they are efficient and effective under the government's system of 'best value', and have been given public service agreements, specifying in detail the outputs that are required of them (*The Guardian*, 2 April 2001, p 17). Comprehensive performance assessment results have led to local authorities and individual departments being given a grading of excellent, good, fair, weak or poor (*The Guardian*, 12 December 2002, p 13). Top-performing authorities in these assessments have been promised greater freedom from central government, while poor performers are likely to face teams being sent in to improve the quality of services (*The Guardian*, 4 December 2002, p 13).

In the case of local authority housing departments (and housing associations), best value has been incorporated into a system of comprehensive performance assessment undertaken by the Audit Commission, which classifies housing services according to a three-star scoring system (*Inside Housing*, 26 July 2002, p 35). One incentive for an authority to achieve an excellent or good rating is that they may then have the opportunity to form an ALMO, as discussed in Chapter One. The creation of an ALMO facilitates the raising of private finance to improve the housing stock.

The development of a rigorous regime of performance assessment may have discouraged authorities from developing services for tenants that go beyond the provision of housing. While it is relatively easy to measure performance in terms of void re-let times (the time taken to re-let a property after the previous tenant has left) and level of rent arrears, measuring the benefits of support services is much more difficult and is likely to require a research study such as the one discussed in this book. An additional difficulty noted by Franklin (1998, pp 201-2) is that housing management has traditionally been seen as consisting of practical, administrative activities – such as allocating empty housing, rent collection and maintenance – with no consensus as to whether broader tasks, such as advice and counselling, should fall within its role. Franklin and Clapham (1997, p 14) suggest that compulsory competitive tendering, combined with the increasing disadvantage of local authority tenants as a result of residualisation, heightened tensions over the appropriate role for housing managers to play:

> Indeed, local authority housing managers are caught in a difficult dilemma as to whether to stave off potential competitors by adopting a basic commercial/contractual service, or serve the perceived needs of tenants in acceding to the legitimisation of a social welfare role, perhaps in the hope that they will be seen as the best agencies to perform such a role.

Despite the support of successive governments for policies designed to measure the work of housing managers more closely, there has also been some encouragement to adopt a broader role with less easily measurable benefits. The Housing Corporation has urged housing associations to adopt an approach described as Housing Plus in acknowledgement that tenancy management cannot be separated from the needs of the wider community (The Housing Corporation, 1997, p 5). The government has promoted the concept of 'neighbourhood management', where local authorities work with agencies such as the police to take an integrated approach to meeting the needs of disadvantaged areas (SEU, 2000b). However, although the Social Exclusion Unit's policy action team report on housing management acknowledged that meeting the needs of disadvantaged areas required more than conventional housing management services, it argued that the role of the housing manager should be to encourage action on the part of other agencies (DETR, 1999b). The report also confirmed that 'core business' tasks would remain central to housing management (DETR, 1999b).

The argument advanced by the housing management report supports the view of Walker (2000, pp 289-91) that the debate about the role of the housing manager has now swung towards a focus on "core business", centred around the collection of rents, the allocation of homes and the maintenance of the stock, all of which help to secure the financial position of the organisation. Walker (2000, p 291) claims that this emphasis is frustrating for housing managers who wish to spend time on activities such as chatting with tenants, which do not produce tangible organisational benefits.

The tension between the role that some housing managers would ideally like to adopt and the one that they feel will provide measurable benefits was evident in Harding's (1999) study of local authority officers who were responsible for dealing with youth homelessness. Officers suggested that, in addition to difficulties in accessing and furnishing accommodation, a variety of other factors were responsible for homelessness: for example, tensions within step-parent families, lifestyle conflicts with neighbours and budgeting problems. However, the actions taken by authorities consisted largely of providing practical help to young homeless people to find housing and furniture. Harding (1999, pp 66-8) suggests two reasons for the differences between beliefs and actions: there were some areas that officers felt were not properly the responsibility of the housing department (so they might, for example, concentrate on providing furniture rather than preventing family breakdown) and there were a limited number of initiatives that could combine concern for the homeless person with meeting 'housing management' objectives. For example, six authorities were letting, or considering letting, larger properties to single people, but in four cases this initiative was restricted to hard-to-let areas.

Other recent policy developments at a local and national level have demonstrated a preference for measures that improve the landlord's housing management performance. Harding and Keenan (1998) argue that the provision of part-furnished accommodation by Newcastle City Council – an initiative which is discussed further later in this chapter – has met the needs of tenants and also those of the local authority by increasing the average length of tenancies. On a larger scale, the number of statutorily homeless households placed temporarily in bed and breakfast hotels in Great Britain fell sharply from 1991 to the mid-1990s (ONS, 2001, p 182), partly due to the development of schemes to lease property from the private rented sector (DoE, 1997). The reduction in the use of bed and breakfast accommodation seems to have arisen both from concern over the conditions in such accommodation (as described by Conway, 1988) and because private sector leasing schemes imposed lower costs on authorities (see *Roof*, July and August 1994, p 25).

The use of bed and breakfast hotels has increased again in recent years, but at a slower rate than the increase in all forms of temporary accommodation (ONS, 2001, p 182). Reducing the use of bed and breakfast accommodation is a key target that the government has set local authorities in the area of homelessness, together with sharp reductions in the number of rough sleepers. Authorities have also been invited, or in some cases required, to set at least one additional target from the following list: reducing levels of repeat homelessness, reducing levels of homelessness against main causes and reducing inappropriate use of temporary accommodation (Homelessness Directorate, 2003, p 3). Again, meeting these targets should ensure that better services are provided to homeless people, but will also reduce the costs that homelessness imposes on local authorities.

The next section will demonstrate the effect of the switch to a 'performance' culture in the areas of housing and services to homeless people in Newcastle. The local authority followed the pattern of other Labour-controlled councils in the 1980s by taking measures to reduce the difficulties experienced by disadvantaged groups such as young people living independently. More recent initiatives, while still aimed at meeting needs, have also emphasised the need to improve housing management performance by producing measurable benefits for the authority.

Responding to homelessness in Newcastle

There follows a selective history of the development of services for young people living independently in Newcastle, focusing on the thinking and motives behind different initiatives. For ease of reference, a glossary is provided here:

Glossary of services provided to young people in Newcastle at the time of the research

Banbury Road – a local authority-owned block of flats for young people, intensively supported by an estate officer and a Single Person's Advice Team worker.

Cumberland House – a hostel for homeless women run by Norcare.

First Move – a team created to find new methods of providing support to young people living independently, which became part of the Newcastle Independence Network.

Gill Street – local authority-owned accommodation for young people with support provided by four Community Service Volunteers.

In Line – part of the Children's Society, this organisation leased self-contained accommodation from the local authority under a management agreement.

Leaving Care Support Team (LCST) – a social services department team that formed part of the Newcastle Independence Network.

Newcastle Independence Network (NIN) – an organisation incorporating the local authority's Leaving Care Support Team and a number of services run by Barnardo's: First Move, the Support Needs Assessment Project and the Start up Team.

Single Person's Advice Team (SPAT), formerly the Single Person's Support Service (SPSS) – the first local authority service developed to provide support to single people living independently.

Start up Scheme – also part of the Newcastle Independence Network, a project that found accommodation for young clients and supported them through the early stages of their tenancy.

Support Needs Assessment Project (SNAP) – a project that formed part of the Newcastle Independence Network and made joint assessments of young people's housing and support needs.

Tyneside Foyer – a project combining accommodation for young people with on-site support to help find employment and training.

Initiatives developed in Newcastle have tended not to focus on providing access to accommodation for two reasons: the apparent surplus of accommodation in the city and the generous treatment of homeless people (particularly young homeless people) through the local authority's allocations system. It was noted previously that the authority was one of the first to treat 16- and 17-year-olds as being in priority need under the homelessness legislation – this development occurred two decades before the 2002 Homelessness (Priority Need for Accommodation) (England) Order made such an approach compulsory for all local authorities.

A sympathetic response to homeless people of all ages was demonstrated by Newcastle's response to the 1996 Housing Act, through which the Conservative government sought to give higher priority to waiting list applicants and lower priority to homeless households, as discussed in Chapter Two. Like many other authorities (see Cloke et al, 2000), Newcastle adjusted its procedures to seek to ensure that homeless people were not disadvantaged by this legislative change. The number of points available for "insecurity of tenure" on the housing register was increased so that more homeless households could be rehoused via the register, without having to be classed as statutorily homeless and move into temporary accommodation (NCC, 1996a).

Whether as a result of this 'reclassification' of homeless people, or of declining demand for housing in the city, a report to the Housing Committee on 9 December 1998 noted that the number of people presenting themselves as homeless had reduced significantly in the previous few years. However, the report commented that:

> of those that do present as homeless, a growing proportion display an increasingly broad and more complex range of needs with homelessness being only one facet of a multiply disadvantaged lifestyle. (NCC, 1998a)

The local authority has identified street homelessness and rough sleeping as relatively small-scale problems within Newcastle. Homeless people with multiple problems are thought to be more likely to experience a nomadic existence, moving between emergency accommodation and the floors of friends and acquaintances, sleeping rough occasionally when these options are not available (NCC, 1998b).

This analysis of homelessness in the city has led the local authority to concentrate its services less on providing access to housing and more on meeting the 'extra' needs of homeless people. These services, particularly the ones for young people, have followed the pattern identified by Gilroy (1993) in addressing both material hardship and support needs. The authority's commitment to meeting material needs appeared to be initially motivated by a desire to oppose Conservative cuts to the welfare state. For example, a report on the effects of the 1988 Social Security Act[1] (NCC, 1988b) argued that:

> there is clearly an unmet need for advice to and support of young single people in helping to meet their accommodation needs. The potential to meet such advice and support needs is constrained principally by the resources available. The need has been compounded by the current round of legislative changes.... One of the most worrying consequences of the benefit changes

has been to push young people into desperate poverty, the effect of which will be to increasingly force people into debt.

The Single Person's Support Service

The first service developed to meet the needs of young people living independently was the Single Person's Support Service (SPSS), which was created in 1983 and initially consisted of three advice workers. Its remit was to provide services to all single people, but particularly 16- and 17-year-olds who were accepted as statutorily homeless (NCC, 1982).

Although the scheme offered support in developing the skills needed for independent living, its key role was to combat poverty:

> The support offered is available both before and after re-housing in order to prepare an individual for the difficulties of establishing a home and assist in maintaining it for a short while. Help is available in the routine tasks of cooking, cleaning, shopping, etcetera. But the majority of assistance requested has been for advice and assistance in problems involving income maintenance and furniture. (NCC, 1984)

A subsequent evaluation confirmed that the main task of the service was welfare rights work, followed by advice about the move from temporary to permanent housing. Some of the early achievements of the service were identified as supporting young people in making successful claims for single payments and applications to charitable trusts (NCC, 1985).

So dealing with structural disadvantage was the key concern in the early years of the SPSS. By the time of the research described in this book, the scheme had expanded to six workers and had been renamed the Single Person's Advice Team (SPAT), although it continued to perform a similar role in supporting single people, particularly young people.

Temporary accommodation

The development of services for people living in local authority temporary accommodation was another measure designed to meet the needs of a highly disadvantaged group, although there has been a stronger focus on personal characteristics in this case. Of the young people in the sample, 21 stayed in the local authority's main block of temporary accommodation at Hill Court and only one stayed at the alternative hostel at New Bridge Street, where access was restricted to female-headed households. The high levels of disadvantage that were noted among sample members who stayed in local authority temporary accommodation have also been observed among people of all ages staying at Hill Court. According to information provided by the temporary accommodation manager, 99% of households arriving at Hill Court in 1998 were unwaged, 70% of 16- and 17-year-olds were on nil income, 36% of residents had drug or alcohol problems and 24% had current or previous contact with psychiatric services.

Until 1989, Hill Court was run with minimal welfare support and a resident caretaker. Early developments in the provision of services were the introduction of 24-hour staffing and closed-circuit television for security purposes. By 1999, services had expanded much further to include emergency cash and food on arrival, 24-hour emergency health cover, an on-site community psychiatric nurse, crèche and childcare facilities, transport, benefits advice and resettlement support to people moving into permanent housing.

The range of services available in temporary accommodation, the speed with which offers of permanent tenancies could be made (due to falling demand for housing) and the reduced number of statutorily homeless households all meant that the local authority had virtually eliminated the use of bed and breakfast accommodation by the time of the research. A total of 95% of statutorily homeless households who required temporary accommodation could be housed in either Hill Court or New Bridge Street. Of the remaining 5%, most could be accommodated by voluntary sector projects: local authority support for voluntary organisations amounted to £318,000 every year (personal communication with a member of the Community and Housing Directorate, 14 March 2003).

The provision of furniture

One of the measures that facilitated a quick move from temporary to permanent accommodation was the provision of furniture. Rooney (1997) noted that Newcastle City Council was the only large-scale local authority provider of furnished lettings in England. The need of young people for furniture was identified in the early stages of the work of the SPSS (NCC, 1985) and this need was reported to have increased as a result of the changes brought about by the 1986 Social Security Act, which replaced single payments with the Social Fund (NCC, 1989). However, the first major development in this area was not designed to meet the needs of young people specifically but consisted of the purchase of second-hand furniture for households in temporary accommodation who had been offered a permanent tenancy. A report to the Special Needs Joint Sub-Committee (NCC, 1990a) noted the benefits of this measure for both homeless households and the local authority itself:

> In addition to causing considerable distress to the individuals, the lack of furniture necessitates the extended use of temporary accommodation. This can contribute, both directly and indirectly, to considerable bed and breakfast expenditure.

The first successful scheme to provide furniture to a wider tenant group was a small initiative involving 25 fully furnished tenancies in multi-storey blocks of flats in Cruddas Park. The provision of furniture occurred at the same time as improvements to security services in the blocks, which had previously been difficult to let. Closed-circuit television was introduced as part of an estate action scheme and 24-hour security porter services were provided. The 1990/ 91 Housing Annual Report noted that this security programme appeared to have resulted in improvements to the authority's management performance, with fewer voids, increased allocations and a greater tenancy life within the blocks. Furniture also seemed to be playing a part: 20 other furnished units were to be introduced as a result of high demand for this type of accommodation (NCC, 1991a).

Concierge services were subsequently introduced to a number of other multi-storey blocks in a variety of locations (NCC, 1994b) and there was also a rapid growth in the provision of furniture. A pilot scheme began in April 1992, offering part-furnished tenancies across the city to new tenants who would otherwise have no means of obtaining furniture. The furniture package consisted of the minimum necessary in order to move in (NCC, 1992) and was provided for a service charge of £7.00 per week for singles and £9.00 per week for other households (Harding and Keenan, 1998, p 383)[2].

A report to the Housing Committee in October 1992 noted that there were financial risks to the local authority in providing dispersed part-furnished units, but again argued that provision could benefit both landlord and tenant:

> ... the review of the small number of furnished units piloted in different parts of the city indicates that we are likely to see the same benefits in terms of tenant satisfaction, ability to make a success of a tenancy and reduced turnover as we are receiving from the fully furnished accommodation provided in the Cruddas Park blocks. (NCC, 1992)

It was reported to the Housing Committee on 10 April 1996 that there were 2,500 local authority part-furnished tenancies (NCC, 1996b). A further report to the Housing Committee on 11 December 1996 argued for this number to increase to 3,500, emphasising the housing management benefits to the authority, particularly the rising average length of part-furnished tenancies (NCC, 1996c). The data collected in this research suggested that a part-furnished tenancy had become the norm for a 16- or 17-year-old rehoused as homeless, as will be shown later in this chapter.

First Move

Another major step in the development of services was the creation of a team named First Move, partly as a result of reports of management problems caused by care leavers living in independent tenancies (NCC, 1990b). A proposal was put to the Special Needs Joint Sub-Committee on 17 September 1991 to create a new system of support for young people moving to live independently from their family or from the care of the social services department. The proposal was made in a report suggesting that existing arrangements were problematic for both young people and the local authority:

> Young people tend to present special problems both for housing and social services. Social services see young people leaving care or leaving home without support who become especially vulnerable both socially and materially. Many of these young people carry profound emotional distress. Some have had a lamentably negative experience of care. Housing policy allows the allocation of tenancies to all of these young people from 16 years onwards but in common with social services, housing have been unable to prevent many of these tenancies failing and the resultant homelessness. Regrettably these young people whilst clearly most in need of support and advice are frequently least able to access appropriate services. The move to independence is all too often premature and in itself an expression of other problems. (NCC, 1991b)

Although this quote implies that young people's inexperience and their family background are to blame for difficulties in independent living, the report also acknowledged the difficulties created by the 1988 Social Security Act. The report recommended that a bid be made to central government for funding for development workers who would identify suitable locations for housing for young people in different parts of the city and develop new support services. The bid for funding was successful and the First Move team was created.

In Line

Despite concerns that young people could present difficulties in housing management terms, the role adopted by advice workers to this point had primarily been advocacy and support based on the needs of the tenant. However, local authority support for the creation of a team named In Line (consisting of staff employed by the Children's Society) represented a move towards a role that combined support with management, intended to meet the needs of both tenant and landlord. A review of supported housing in 1997 proposed that In Line should lease 40 flats from the local authority or housing associations; the tenants should be homeless 16- and 17-year-olds who had significant behavioural problems, or exhibit antisocial behaviour, and require very long-term flexible support and befriending if their behaviour is to be changed for the better (NCC, 1997).

This recommendation was accepted and, at the time of the research, In Line had begun to form management agreements with the local authority to take on tenancies on behalf of young people.

Factors influencing service development

This brief history demonstrates how the focus of services has changed with time. This is perhaps most clearly illustrated by the different reasons that were given by the local authority for establishing the SPSS in the 1980s and for supporting In Line in the late 1990s. The rapid expansion of furniture provision can also be seen as indicative of a growing preference for services that meet the needs of disadvantaged people while improving the housing management performance of the local authority. Similarly, although services provided at Hill Court were focused on the needs of the most vulnerable tenants, meeting these needs effectively could facilitate a quicker move to permanent accommodation and so indirectly reduce costs for the authority. However, it should be noted that the introduction of services has not always been a reflection of a single approach – this point is particularly well illustrated by the range of reasons given for creating the First Move team. Material needs, failings in informal support and personal shortcomings have all featured as reasons for introducing services in Newcastle.

Services available to young people at the time of the research

Before evaluating the services received by the sample, it may be helpful to briefly summarise the range of provision for young people at the time of the research. The city council was the chief provider of permanent accommodation to 16- and 17-year-olds, with a very small number of lettings being made to this age group by housing associations and private landlords. Accommodation with on-site support designated for young people was provided by the council at sites in Banbury Road (North Kenton) and Gill Street (Benwell). At Banbury Road a block of 15 flats had 24-hour porterage and intensive support from an estate officer and a SPAT worker. At Gill Street a block of eight fully furnished flats was given 24-hour support by four Community Service Volunteers, with two living on site and two in a nearby street (NCC, 1994c; and personal contact with a member of the Community and Housing Directorate, 17 June 2003).

Support for tenants of general purpose local authority accommodation was provided by the six members of SPAT (employed by the local authority) and by First Move (whose workers were employed by Barnardo's). First Move had by now joined with a number of other voluntary projects to form the Newcastle Independence Network (NIN). The other parts of the Network included:

• The Leaving Care Support Team (LCST), consisting of staff of Newcastle's social services department. This team provided a range of support services to facilitate the transition to independence of 15- to 21-year-olds who were, or had been, in care in the city (NIN, 1999). The LCST continued to provide many of the services that had originally been established within the social services department: for example, a 15+ team that offered extra social work contact beyond the age where the local authority's legal obligation ended[3] and a fostering scheme that found placements for a range of young people aged over 15, to prevent them from moving into independence before they were ready (NCC, 1997). The LCST also offered young people in care services such as advice, befriending and a preparation for leaving care group (NIN, 1999).

- The Start up Scheme provided one-to-one support to people aged 16-25 who were homeless or threatened with homelessness and who required intensive support to make a success of independent living. The scheme sought to provide access to accommodation for clients and flexible temporary support in the early stages of their tenancy (NIN, 1999).
- The Support Needs Assessment Project (SNAP) offered a joint housing and support needs assessment to young people who had approached the homeless section or another part of the housing department. After making the assessment, the project worked in partnership with other agencies, such as housing and social services, to seek to ensure that appropriate support was offered in the move to independent living. It also offered group work to enable young people to develop independent living skills (NIN, 1999).

Information sources about agency services

Information about the services received by the sample was obtained through the records of the agencies that had contact with them and by asking specific questions of those young people who were interviewed. This information was collected in order to establish the types of support that were most commonly being provided, to determine whether some groups of young people were receiving more support than others and to show whether there were particular support services that could increase the likelihood of achieving success in a tenancy.

Agencies that were asked about their contacts with young people were the homeless section, the NIN, the SPAT team and In Line. Agency records were the preferred method of data collection because they were assumed to be more accurate than young people's own recollections on issues such as the number of contacts. However, there were too many neighbourhood housing and social services offices to contact individually, so young people themselves were asked about support provided from these sources. The first and second interview schedules also included questions about the sample's contact with First Move, as it was thought at the start of the research that this was the 'specialist' service that would reach most young people. There was also a question about support from other, unspecified organisations to seek to determine whether the range of agencies that had had contact with the sample was greater than had originally been envisaged. Responses to this question demonstrated that young people had very little contact with agencies other than those discussed earlier.

Asking young people themselves about the services they had received had advantages in terms of ascertaining their opinion of these services. However, this approach also presented a number of difficulties – most obviously, there were only 94 first interview respondents, and 45 second interview respondents, compared to a total sample size of 145. In addition, anecdotal evidence suggested that young people were unable to distinguish between services provided by housing managers and those delivered by SPAT workers, so respondents were asked questions about the work of the housing department without distinguishing between these two sections. A further difficulty emerged when it became clear that some sample members were not reporting contact with the housing or social services departments as 'help' – possibly because it was not perceived to be helpful. As a result, later respondents were asked two sets of questions: one about 'help from', and one about 'contact with', housing and social services.

Findings

The homeless application was the first contact that most sample members had with any service provider: just 34 of the 145 (23.4%) had any involvement with agencies prior to this point. The application tended to be made at an early stage of the young person's housing career: only 11 first interview respondents (11.7%) had left home and then returned, and only three had been living away from home or care for a year or more before approaching the homeless section. So agencies had the opportunity to work with a large majority of the young people before they experienced the damaging consequences of long-term homelessness identified by Hutson and Liddiard (1991, pp 36-9). However, the research showed that there were major difficulties in reaching the sample with the extensive network of services that was available.

The provision of services in temporary accommodation

Although 19 first interview respondents had stayed at Hill Court, only seven said that they had received advice and support during their stay. Four reported receiving financial or benefits advice, while social activities, advice on other places to stay, the provision of money and a food pack were all mentioned by one respondent.

The reason for this low reported take up of services was unclear. One possible explanation is that respondents took a narrow view of the question about 'advice or support' and did not see services such as transport to their accommodation as fitting this term.

The seven young people who said that they had received advice or support mainly viewed it positively. Three reported that it was very helpful, three that it was quite helpful and only one that it was not helpful at all.

Table 4.1: Tenure of property to which young people rehoused

Property rehoused to	Frequency	%
Council tenancy	130	89.7
In Line tenancy	5	4.1
Gill Street	4	2.8
Cumberland House	3	2.1
Banbury Road	2	1.4
Foyer	1	0.7
Total	145	100.0

Long-term housing

The type of permanent (or semi-permanent) housing that young people were rehoused into is shown in Table 4.1.

Cumberland House and the Tyneside Foyer were not originally involved in the research, so the information collected about the young people who moved into these two settings was less extensive than for the remainder of the sample. However, Cumberland House provided information about all three of the young women who lived there: one who left after completing a resettlement programme was judged to have succeeded in independent living, but two who left under less favourable circumstances were judged to have failed. In the case of the young person who moved into the Tyneside Foyer, they had moved on by the time that the interviewer called for the first interview, so it was assumed that their stay had been unsuccessful.

For all the young people, the type of support service they received was partly dependent on the tenure of property to which they were rehoused. The SPAT team did not contact young people who moved into Gill Street or In Line tenancies because of the availability of other workers to provide support. In addition, the tenants of Gill Street had no need for furniture packages because the accommodation was fully furnished.

The provision of furniture

As can be seen from Table 4.1, a total of 137 young people moved into In Line tenancies, Banbury Road or other council tenancies. Data were available about the level of furnishing at which 133 of these properties were let: 26 tenancies (19.5%) were unfurnished, 103 (77.4%) were part-furnished and four (3.0%) were fully furnished. The 94 first interview respondents were asked about the extent to which they received help with finding items of furniture from sources other than the local authority. A total of 53 (56.4%) received such assistance: the people most likely to help were relatives (in 37 cases) followed by friends (in 17). Respondents who got on badly with their family were particularly unlikely to receive help with furniture from informal sources ($p=0.095$).

Despite the help available from the local authority and other sources, 45 respondents (47.9%) said that their accommodation lacked furniture. All four

Table 4.2: Items of furniture respondents were lacking

Item of furniture	Frequency
Carpets	24
Settee	17
Fridge-freezer/fridge	10
Washing machine	7
Curtains	7
Bedcovers	4
Wallpaper	4
Bed/new bed	3
Cutlery	3
Chairs	3
Cooker/cooking equipment	2
Crockery	2

tenants with fully furnished tenancies felt that their property was adequately furnished, but the answers given to this question by respondents in part-furnished and unfurnished accommodation were very similar: approximately half of each group considered that they were without essential items. Asked which items were missing, seven respondents said everything or almost everything. The number of times that specific items were listed by other respondents is shown in Table 4.2.

The picture changed little when considering only those respondents with part-furnished tenancies: carpets, a settee and a fridge or fridge-freezer were still the items of furniture identified as missing most often.

There was some evidence to suggest that difficulties with furniture tended to ease with time. Ten second interview respondents (22.2%) said that they lacked essential items, compared to 17 of the 45 who had said this at the time of the first interview. The only specific item of furniture identified as lacking by more than one second interview respondent was carpets (in four cases).

When considering the impact of furniture on the experience of independent living, the extent to which respondents experienced financial difficulties appeared to be unrelated to whether their tenancy was fully furnished, part-furnished or unfurnished. In addition, across the sample as a whole, the level of furnishing had no impact on the outcome of tenancies. However, a different pattern emerged when considering the lone parents only: both lone parents rehoused into unfurnished accommodation failed in their tenancies, compared to two of the 14 who were rehoused into part-furnished accommodation ($p=0.005$). So, for this particular group, the provision of furniture seemed to produce a lasting benefit for both tenant and landlord.

Support provided by non-specialist agencies

When considering the findings about young people's relationship with the housing and social services departments, the methodological difficulties noted earlier should be borne in mind. Respondents appeared to be more likely to be in touch with the housing department, with 65 (69.1%) reporting help and/or contact at the first interview. The 'help' provided was mainly in the form of one-off, material assistance: 17 respondents said that they were expecting or had received a decorating allowance, 15 mentioned the furniture pack and six discussed some form of advice about benefits. Of the 43 respondents who reported receiving assistance, 36 (83.7%) said that it was very helpful or quite helpful. In contrast, 'contact' was often about routine tenancy matters and was not perceived so positively: 10 respondents complained that the speed of repairs was too slow.

Only 16 of the 94 first interview respondents (17.0%) reported receiving help from, or having contact with, the social services department. The help and contact was frequently in relation to material needs (for example, the provision of food vouchers) and was mainly perceived to be helpful. The satisfaction that the sample expressed with material forms of assistance seems entirely consistent with the concerns over financial matters that were highlighted in the previous chapter.

Support provided by specialist agencies

The homelessness application should have resulted in a number of services being provided by those agencies whose work was discussed earlier in the chapter. However, take up of these services was limited, possibly due to the initial confidence that the sample felt about independent living. The extent to which respondents had had contact with key agencies – and had received traditional benefits/advocacy services – is illustrated by Table 4.3.

The apparently low take up of In Line services was explained by this agency only beginning to offer tenancies towards the end of the study. In Line was the agency that provided the most intensive support to its clients. Of the five young people who took up their tenancies, one failed to attend any appointments and was subsequently evicted. All four of the others were visited weekly or more frequently, all were offered advice/assistance with fuel connections or payments and all were advised about their tenancy conditions or rent obligations. Other subjects on which advice or assistance were provided by In Line included budgeting (in three cases), health (in two), personal safety (in two) and travel (in two).

Table 4.3: Respondents' contact with agencies

Agency	Number of respondents in contact	Number of respondents provided with benefits/ financial advice	Number of respondents assisted with Social Fund applications
SPAT	105 (72.4%)	50	21
SNAP	53 (36.6%)	33	0
First Move	22 (15.2%)	9	9
In Line	5 (3.4%)	4	4

Seven respondents had been offered assistance by First Move but had refused it. The low take up of the services offered by this agency was particularly disappointing because, among the 17 first interview respondents who evaluated help received, the view taken was mainly a positive one. Four said that First Move had been very helpful, 11 that it had been quite helpful, one that they did not need help and one that they did not yet know how helpful the assistance had been. In addition to advice/assistance with benefits or finance, other frequently provided services were advice/assistance with furniture or money for furniture (in nine cases) and assistance with applications to charities (in five).

The Start up Scheme does not appear in Table 4.3 because the scheme seemed to have little contact with sample members, although it should be remembered that its remit was to work intensively with a relatively small number of young people. One sample member had been contacted by the scheme to see how they were getting on, one discussed financial problems with a scheme worker and one had a general chat. In all three cases this contact was rated as quite helpful by the young person.

The SPAT workers had an advantage over other agencies in seeking to make contact with young people because they arranged the furniture package for tenants of part-furnished accommodation and so tended to see them at the point when they signed their tenancy agreement. In the majority of cases, there was only one contact between the SPAT worker and the sample member. However, the SPAT team were able to provide advice or assistance with fuel connections or payments to 47 (or 44.8%) of their 105 clients and advice on tenancy conditions or rent obligations to 39 (or 37.1%).

When combining the information about the work of the different agencies, it is clear that – although take up of services was limited – the types of support provided had developed substantially beyond a basic benefits/advocacy function. Of the 145 sample members:

- 51 (35.2%) were given advice or assistance with fuel connections or payments by SPAT or In Line;
- 43 (29.7%) were provided with advice about tenancy conditions or rent obligations by SPAT or In Line;
- 14 (9.7%) received help in finding extra furniture from SPAT, In Line or First Move; and
- 12 (8.3%) received assistance with applications to charities from SPAT, In Line or SNAP.

The number of respondents being advised about tenancy conditions or rent obligations suggests that the need to protect the landlord's interests was also becoming a feature of support services, even among the SPAT team, who historically had worked to a very clear advocacy agenda.

It was suggested earlier that one reason for the low take up of services may have been the confidence that young people felt about independent living.

However, 16 first interview respondents (17.0%) said that they thought they would need some special help in their tenancy. Of these 16, 11 wanted help from the social services department, two from the housing department, one from a doctor, one from the LCST and in one case the preferred source of help was not indicated. In 13 cases the type of assistance required was specified – 10 respondents wanted special help in the form of furniture or financial help. The desire for material support may have been linked to this group being more likely to be in debt than the remainder of the sample ($p=0.041$). However, they were also a group who tended to have received more services than other sample members – they were more likely to have been assisted to find furniture ($p=0.089$), more likely to have had four or more contacts with the SPAT team ($p=0.052$) and more likely to have had help from, or contact with, the social services department ($p=0.005$).

The group who desired special help were particularly likely to fail in their tenancies ($p=0.093$). This finding suggests that, while it may be difficult to persuade young people to use services in most cases, there are some who desire and need very intensive support.

Services and disadvantaged groups

There was little evidence of the disadvantage of some groups of young people being compensated for by greater contact with agencies. Indeed, the opposite pattern applied in some cases: a number of services were more likely to be taken up by respondents who had low scores on the index of social problems. Although the relationships between variables were sometimes complex, it appeared that respondents with none of the problems on the index were particularly likely to have been offered help to find extra furniture by SPAT or In Line workers ($p=0.068$), to have contact with First Move ($p=0.081$) and to report help or contact with the housing department ($p=0.044$). In addition, the seven respondents who did not have a GP were particularly likely to have high numbers of problems ($p=0.021$). The only finding to present a different pattern was that young people who had been in trouble with the police were more likely to report receiving help from the social services department ($p=0.012$).

The evidence in relation to two of the other disadvantaged groups was mixed. Men were less likely to have had contact with the SPAT team than young women ($p=0.037$), but more likely to report receiving help from the social services department ($p=0.014$). Respondents who had stayed in local authority temporary accommodation were particularly likely to have agencies supporting them at the time of their homeless application ($p=0.058$), but particularly unlikely to be assessed by SNAP ($p=0.049$).

Services provided to care leavers

In contrast to the broader picture, it appeared that young people who had been in local authority care were making substantial use of the services that were available to them. Of the nine care leavers interviewed at the first stage, five reported receiving help from the social services department: a statistically greater proportion than for the sample as a whole ($p=0.002$). It was possible that there was no clear distinction in respondents' minds between social services and the LCST, although two respondents who reported receiving assistance from social services also said that they had been helped by the LCST. In one of these cases a respondent had been advised about moving in and in the other the LCST member had advised them about bills, made sure that they had enough to eat and said that they were available if needed. Both respondents were very satisfied with the support received.

Of the four care leavers who did not report receiving help from the social services department, one had met with the Start up Scheme and one reported contact with both the social services department and the Start up Scheme. However, some services were no more likely to have contact with care leavers than with other young people. One care leaver was rehoused into Cumberland House and, of the remaining eight, four reported help from or contact with the housing department, none had First Move contact, one was assessed by SNAP and six had contact with the SPAT team, with two having more than one contact.

In addition to noting the level of contact with agencies, a further method of evaluation of the services provided to care leavers was to ask them how involved they had been in their plan to leave care. Four said that they were very involved, one that they were quite involved, two that they were not very involved and two that they were not involved at all. Although this may seem disappointing, it represents an improvement on the findings of Kirby (1994, p 6) that less than one third of a sample of homeless care leavers felt that they had discussed a clear plan about when they would leave care and where they would live.

Care leavers were more likely than the remainder of the sample to have high numbers of social problems ($p=0.041$). However, there were no statistically significant differences in their experience of independent living when compared to other respondents. Five of the nine care leavers succeeded in their tenancy – a similar proportion to that observed in the sample as a whole.

The high level of contact with the social services department, the relatively positive view of the process of planning to leave care and the extent of success in tenancies among care leavers are all strands of evidence to suggest that the services developed in Newcastle have been effective in meeting needs. This finding was supported by considering the percentage of sample members (9.6%) who had been in local authority care. This is an overrepresentation when considering that approximately 1% of all young people have experience of the care system. However, studies have suggested that this overrepresentation is much more severe in other areas: government figures for 1999 suggested that a quarter of the people sleeping rough in London were care leavers (*The Guardian*, 10 September 2002, p 67), while the Scottish Executive (2002, p 6) estimates that between 20 and 50% of young homeless people in Scotland have been in the care of local authorities.

Impact of services

While the extent to which services were reaching young people – particularly the most disadvantaged young people – is clearly an important issue, the key justification for providing services must be that they produce positive effects. As many services were focused on material needs, the effect that they had on the sample's experience of debt was examined. However, the most important level of evaluation was the impact of services on tenancy outcomes.

The findings provided a very mixed picture in relation to the effect of services on the experience of debt. Respondents who were in debt at the first interview were more likely than other sample members to report receiving help from the social services department ($p=0.029$), but less likely to say that they had been provided with assistance by the housing department ($p=0.028$). These findings are open to different interpretations: they could indicate that social services were more effective in reaching young people in the greatest need, or that help from the housing department was more effective in preventing debt. Agency records showed that first interview respondents who had debts were more likely to have received benefits advice ($p=0.092$) but less likely to receive assistance in making charity applications ($p=0.094$). However, since these services may have been provided after the first interview, it is difficult to determine cause and effect.

The 'sequence of events' was more obvious when using the variable that separated the respondents who had acquired debts between the first and second interviews from those who had remained debt free. The difficulty here was that the numbers involved tended not to be large enough to establish statistical significance, so the findings can only be used as indicators of patterns that may exist on a larger scale. Respondents who had acquired new debts by the time of the second interview were particularly likely to have received a number of services, that is, they were more likely to have been:

- given benefits advice;
- assisted to find extra items of furniture;
- assisted to make Social Fund applications by SPAT or In Line workers; and
- assessed by SNAP.

In addition to the lack of statistical significance, these findings again raise issues of interpretation – they could indicate that young people who were slipping into financial difficulties were more likely to contact agencies. However, a clear implication is that agencies should re-examine their services to establish whether they could be more effective in preventing young people from falling into debt.

There were also difficulties in interpretation of the data when considering the effect of a young person's relationship with the housing department on the success or failure of their tenancy. First interview respondents were more likely to fail if they reported receiving help from the housing department ($p=0.096$) and, equally surprisingly, more likely to fail if they rated this assistance as helpful ($p=0.023$). One possible explanation for these findings is that, as most of the 'help' reported was one-off material assistance such as providing furniture or decoration allowances, this form of assistance is more effective in providing immediate tenant satisfaction than in facilitating long-term success in housing. However, the management benefits of providing part-furnished tenancies have repeatedly been established elsewhere and this study confirmed their effectiveness in the case of lone parents. Further research to evaluate the effectiveness of a housing department's contact with young tenants is clearly required, particularly if such research can effectively distinguish between the roles of support workers and housing management staff.

Turning to clearer and more positive effects of services, 19 sample members had no income at the time of first contact with the SPAT team and two In Line tenants were in a similar position at their first meeting with workers. The number of these young people interviewed at the first stage was 16, by which time only two still had no income, as was noted in the previous chapter. Providing access to a regular source of income may be seen as a positive end in itself – particularly as most 16- and 17-year-olds do not have an entitlement to benefit – but this research also suggests indirectly a benefit in terms of tenancy outcomes. This suggestion arises from a comparison of the surprisingly high success rate of the 17 women who had no income at their first contact with SPAT or In Line workers (as shown by Table 3.4 in the previous chapter) with the failure of both the respondents who had no income at the time of the first interview.

The tenure of the property that a respondent was rehoused into – and the support services that they received as a result – also appeared to have an impact

Table 4.4: Cross table of whether tenancy successful by property to which rehoused

		Tenancy successful?		
		Yes	No	Total
Property rehoused to	Council tenancy	73	57	130
	In Line tenancy	4	1	5
	Gill Street	0	4	4
	Cumberland House	1	2	3
	Banbury Road	0	2	2
	Foyer	0	1	1
Total		**78**	**67**	**145**

on tenancy outcomes. Respondents who were rehoused into Gill Street were particularly likely to fail in their tenancies, but those who were given In Line tenancies were more likely than others to succeed (p=0.058) (see Table 4.4).

When considering the young men only, tenure continued to have a significant effect (p=0.089), with all three who stayed at Gill Street failing in their tenancies and both the In Line tenants succeeding.

One possible explanation for the effect of the form of housing and support on tenancy outcomes emerged when making comparisons between those services that were linked to a particular building (Banbury Road, Gill Street, Cumberland House and the Foyer) and those where support could be provided across a variety of locations (In Line and local authority tenancies). Nine of the ten sample members rehoused into a 'fixed' setting failed in their tenancy: a very much higher failure rate than for the sample as a whole (p=0.006).

One difficulty in providing housing and support that is tied to a specific building may be that young people do not have a choice about the area that they live in. Four of the six first interview respondents who were living in a 'fixed' setting said that they did not like the area, compared to six of the 88 who had forms of housing that were not tied to a particular location (p=0.011)[4]. When this finding is considered alongside one from the previous chapter, that liking the area they were living in increased the likelihood that a young person would succeed in their tenancy, one reason for projects in fixed locations experiencing high levels of tenancy failure seems clear.

Despite the primary importance of housing and support services offering a choice of location, the success of the two male In Line tenants was still notable, particularly in the light of the poor tenancy outcomes achieved by the young men across the sample as a whole. Young men also seemed to benefit from contact with the SPAT workers. Although the relationship between tenancy outcomes and the number of SPAT contacts was a complex one, it appeared that male respondents who had no contact at all were less likely to succeed (p=0.088) (see Table 4.5).

It was difficult to find a specific type of advice and support that had a measurable effect on tenancy outcomes. The only clear finding in this area was

Table 4.5: Cross table of whether tenancy successful by number of contacts with SPAT team: men only

		Tenancy successful?		
		Yes	No	Total
Number of contacts with SPAT team	0	2	8	10
	1	8	10	18
	2-3	0	2	2
	4-12	2	0	2
Total		12	20	32

Note: 32 young men are included in this table because only local authority tenants could receive the services of the SPAT team.

---

that respondents who had been advised by SPAT or In Line workers about their tenancy conditions and/or rent obligations were more likely to succeed in their tenancies (p=0.015) (see Table 4.6).

This finding remained statistically significant when considering young women only (p=0.029). It seems consistent with the argument developed in the previous chapter that overconfidence can have a detrimental effect on young women's ability to live independently. The implication appears to be that advice which makes clear the obligations involved in holding a tenancy may be an effective method of ensuring that a realistic view is taken.

However, although a number of variables relating to support services were shown to have a statistically significant effect on tenancy outcomes, discriminant analysis suggested that their impact was not as great as the characteristics and circumstances of the young people that were discussed in the previous chapter. On the list of 18 variables with a statistically significant impact on the tenancy outcomes of the sample as a whole, tenure of property rehoused to was the twelfth most influential and advice about tenancy conditions or rent obligations was fifteenth. So, although the research could demonstrate benefits from services, it also suggested that their impact on the outcome of young people's tenancies was limited.

Summary

The data discussed in this chapter raise issues about both the coverage and effectiveness of services. The most positive findings were in relation to care leavers: although it was not possible to identify which of the services developed in Newcastle had the greatest effect, the package of measures appeared to be effective in reducing the incidence of homelessness to a lower rate than has been observed in other areas. In addition, care leavers who were rehoused as homeless were as likely as other young people to conduct a successful tenancy.

When considering other disadvantaged groups, many of the 16- and 17-year-olds who stayed at Hill Court appeared not to be accessing the extensive services that were available there. In addition, there was clearly a difficulty for service providers in reaching young people who had experienced social problems

Table 4.6: Cross table of whether tenancy successful by whether SPAT/In Line provided advice on tenancy conditions or rent obligations

		Tenancy successful?		
		Yes	**No**	**Total**
SPAT advice on tenancy	Yes	30	13	**43**
conditions or rent?	No	29	32	**61**
	Offered but not taken up	3	0	**3**
	Not stated	2	0	**2**
Total		64	45	109

such as truancy and crime. Indeed, the only agency that was shown to be concentrating its work on the most disadvantaged sample members was the social services department, which was particularly likely to have contact with young men, people who were in debt, care leavers and young people who had been in trouble with the police. However, although it appeared to target its services effectively, the social services department had contact with only a small number of the sample: the most common type of ongoing agency contact was with the housing department over housing management matters.

There was a more general difficulty with low take up of the extensive range of services that was available in Newcastle. This may have reflected the sample's confidence about independent living and the belief of many of the young people that only material forms of assistance were needed. The data presented in the previous chapter suggest that this confidence was misplaced, so a major question for agencies is how to reach young people with services that they wrongly perceive to be unnecessary. In contrast, a completely different attitude appeared to exist among a minority of the sample who said that they needed special help in their tenancy, despite already having received substantial support in many cases. As these young people were more likely than others to fail in their tenancies, they present another challenge to agencies seeking to provide effective support services.

Considering the types of service that were effective, the finding that young people were less likely to succeed in their tenancies if their housing and support were provided at a fixed location is consistent with the data discussed in the previous chapter. The research clearly demonstrates the benefits of young people having a choice about the area that they live in and feeling positively about that area.

However, the issue of choice raised difficulties when considering the type of support provided to young people. While the preference of the sample was for material forms of assistance, the support that had the clearest benefit in terms of tenancy outcomes – for both the sample as a whole and young women in particular – was advice about tenancy conditions and/or rent obligations. The tension between services that young people desired and those that were shown to have a positive effect will be considered further in the next chapter.

The findings about the different effects of services on young women and young men seem consistent with the broader pattern of gender differences discussed in the previous chapter. Young men being particularly likely to succeed in tenancies if receiving support from the SPAT team, or the intensive contact offered through an In Line tenancy, supports the view that they need reassurance about their ability to live independently. Similarly, young women's increased likelihood of success if advised about tenancy conditions or rent obligations appears consistent with the assumption that they benefit from taking a less optimistic, or more realistic, view of independent living at an early stage.

When considering the historical development of services for young people living independently in Newcastle, these services appear to have followed a broader national picture by focusing on advocacy in the 1980s but subsequently incorporating a greater range of objectives, particularly improving the housing management performance of the local authority itself. The definition of 'success' in a tenancy adopted in this research was based on the landlord's perspective, so it was perhaps unsurprising that those services identified as most effective – advice about tenancy conditions/rent obligations and the combination of tenancy management and support offered by In Line – were those designed to meet the needs of both the tenant and the landlord. However, it was difficult to demonstrate the impact of more traditional, advocacy-based services on even the incidence of debt, suggesting that there is more work to be done to justify these services in an era where quantifiable benefits need to be shown. In this context, the findings about the positive impact of helping young women to access a regular source of benefit income, and of letting part-furnished accommodation to lone parents, are particularly important in providing a rationale for services to meet the material needs of young tenants.

Overall, the research provided only limited evidence of the benefits of services, particularly when comparing their effects to those of young people's personal characteristics and physical circumstances. The response of Newcastle City Council to the findings has been to seek to increase take up of services, but also to build an evidence base to measure the impact of specific forms of advice and support more closely. This response is discussed in the next chapter.

Notes

[1] The Act removed the entitlement of 16- and 17-year-olds to receive means-tested benefits, as discussed in Chapter Two.

[2] This charge was eligible for Housing Benefit so made no difference to the disposable income of most tenants.

[3] This team was created before the 2000 Children (Leaving Care) Act extended the local authority's responsibility beyond the age of 16.

[4] Although some of the 'fixed' projects were in low-demand areas, this did not seem an adequate explanation for this difference: two of the four successful In Line tenants were rehoused into North Kenton (the same neighbourhood as the Banbury Road block), while another was rehoused in Scotswood (one of the lowest-demand neighbourhoods in the city). Only one was rehoused into a neighbourhood with a relatively high demand for housing, namely West Denton.

FIVE

Policy implications for central and local government

This chapter uses the findings from the research to evaluate the government's approach to supporting young people who are living independently, examining both the broad direction of policy and specific measures. It also identifies the implications for other social landlords of the evaluation of the services provided by Newcastle City Council and examines the steps that the local authority has taken to adjust services as a result of the research findings.

As the research was undertaken in one specific case study authority, it is necessary to consider how far the findings can be generalised to other areas. There are distinctive social and economic conditions present in Newcastle: most notably that rented housing is relatively easy for young people to find, but there are particular difficulties in obtaining well-paid employment. It is acknowledged that local authorities, and other organisations with responsibility for rehousing young people, may be operating in a very different context to the one in Newcastle. However, many of the key findings – such as the danger of overconfidence about independent living – seem applicable to any social and economic context.

Social exclusion

Considering first the broad direction of central government policy, the findings suggest that social exclusion is a helpful concept for understanding youth homelessness and the difficulties that many young people experience in independent living. Although the government has been criticised for failing to provide a precise definition of social exclusion, the data demonstrated that the needs of the sample were indeed very wide ranging and went well beyond their original lack of housing. Comparisons between the research data and information that is available about other people of the same age showed that the sample were more likely:

- to have left school without achieving any GCSEs;
- to have truanted from school;
- to smoke; and
- to have been in trouble with the police.

Further support for the view expressed by the Social Exclusion Unit (2001a, p 10) that social problems tend to be linked, and mutually reinforcing, was provided by the evidence of multiple difficulties experienced by some members of the sample, for example:

• Respondents who were taking drugs at the time of the first interview were more likely than others to have achieved no GCSEs, to have truanted from school, to have been in trouble with the police, to be in debt and to find that their relationship with their parents deteriorated with time.
• In addition to being more likely to take drugs, respondents who were in debt at the first interview were also more likely to smoke daily, to have been in trouble with the police, to view their property as being inadequately furnished and to feel that they had not had enough advice about independent living.

The measures that the government has taken to tackle exclusion at the level of the individual young person will be considered in a later section.

Area-based factors

The measures that the government has taken to tackle exclusion at the level of the individual young person are discussed later in this chapter. When considering the geographical aspect, it was noted in Chapter Two that the government's national strategy for neighbourhood renewal incorporates a very wide range of measures and initiatives. This holistic view is in contrast to some previous approaches that have been heavily criticised for concentrating on the most obvious signs of physical decay (Furbey, 1999, p 428). The research findings suggest that the present government's approach is appropriate and that emphasis should be placed on those measures that involve tackling crime and antisocial behaviour. The experience of these activities, or the fear of them, featured heavily in the reasons that a minority of the sample gave for disliking the area that they were living in. They were also key factors in the small number of interviews conducted with young people who had given up tenancies. As dislike of the area was a factor linked to the failure of tenancies, measures to tackle crime and antisocial behaviour would seem to have the potential to improve tenancy outcomes.

The introduction of the neighbourhood warden schemes is one element of the government's renewal strategy that seems particularly likely to benefit young people, because of the focus on reducing crime and the fear of crime (ODPM, 2000). In Newcastle, wardens concentrate on tackling four types of issue: environmental problems, youth disorder, the fear of crime and keeping in touch with vulnerable groups. Although wardens were initially introduced in some of the most disadvantaged wards of the city, there are now plans to employ them across a much wider area (NCC, 2003d). This is important because the research found no link between specific geographical locations and sample members' experience of crime and antisocial behaviour. More generally, the findings offered little evidence to suggest that young people rehoused into low-demand areas faced greater difficulties than others: the only problem that was linked to specific locations was the greater likelihood of falling into debt between the interviews for those young people rehoused into Cruddas Park and Benwell (the two areas of lower-demand for rented housing).

So, when examining the origins of difficulties that young people experienced in their immediate environment, the appropriate focus is not the lowest-demand neighbourhoods, but rather the broader process of residualisation and the trend towards local authorities housing the most disadvantaged people, often with major support needs. However, the city-wide reduction in demand for rented housing may have contributed to the area-based difficulties faced by the sample: falling demand has been argued to be both a cause (for example, Bramley and Pawson, 2002, p 403) and a consequence (Power and Mumford, 1999) of crime and antisocial behaviour. Many Metropolitan authorities are now demolishing parts of their housing stock in an attempt to find a better balance between supply and demand (Bramley and Pawson, 2002, pp 412-13).

In Newcastle, a slightly different approach is being taken by seeking to attract people back into the city through the local authority's Going for Growth strategy. This ambitious approach aims to reverse the long-term decline in levels of employment and the number of people living in the city. Plans include improvements to transport and the creation of jobs, together with the building of more homes of mixed tenure. However, part of the strategy involves the demolition of some of the least popular local authority housing (*The Journal*, 26 June 2003, p 42).

The implementation of the Going for Growth strategy demonstrated difficulties that may arise in any renewal programme that involves demolition. Newcastle City Council faced strong opposition from the local community when seeking to implement plans to demolish 2,000 properties in Scotswood (a low-demand neighbourhood in the Benwell area) (*Newcastle Evening Chronicle*, 7 March 2001, p 17). The local authority has since worked hard to involve communities in decision making and the Going for Growth programme was progressed with much lower levels of conflict (*The Journal*, 26 June 2003, p 42). However, the experience has emphasised the importance of social and community ties, even in the areas with the greatest social problems. The importance of communities was emphasised in the research described in this book, where the most common reason for young people liking the area that they were living in was the proximity to family and friends.

Linked to the Going for Growth strategy is the selection of Newcastle and Gateshead as one of the locations for the government's market renewal Pathfinder projects, which aim to tackle low demand and abandonment in selected areas of the North of England and the Midlands (ODPM, 2003c). These projects are part of a broader government programme to replace obsolete housing in low-demand areas and to build more in areas of shortage. Deputy Prime Minister John Prescott has indicated that changes to housing supply must be matched by changes to other local services:

> Much of the Communities Plan is properly about housing. But sustainable communities need more than just housing. They need a strong economy; jobs; good schools and hospitals; good public transport; a safe and healthy local environment, better design, more sustainable construction, better use of land and much more. (ODPM, 2003d)

The research suggests that "much more" should include preserving and building social support networks. Any changes to housing supply should acknowledge the vital role of such networks, even in areas of low demand.

Choosing where to live

The importance of informal support networks was further emphasised in the research findings by the strong influence of variables related to peer group relationships on tenancy outcomes and, indirectly, by the greater likelihood of success if a young person liked the area they were living in. It was clearly advantageous that over 90% of the sample could be rehoused into their preferred area. While reduced demand for local authority rented housing presents difficulties for housing managers, one positive effect is that accommodation can usually be offered close to support networks.

In common with many other local authorities, Newcastle is currently introducing a choice-based lettings scheme, initially on a pilot basis. These schemes – which involve prospective tenants applying for specific properties rather than being allocated housing by an officer – have been argued to increase applicants' level of choice over where they live, in addition to giving greater transparency to the allocation process (Kullberg, 2002, p 576) and reducing void re-let times (Pollhammer and Grainger, 2003, pp 40-5). Choice-based lettings schemes have been advocated by central government: the Office of the Deputy Prime Minister has set a target of 25% of authorities introducing some form of choice-based lettings by 2005 and all authorities offering choice to applicants by 2010 (ODPM, 2003b).

The impact of such schemes on homeless people is currently an underresearched area. Statutorily homeless households have tended to be given a time-limited period in which they will be given priority for any suitable property that they apply for: a time limit of three months has been applied during the pilot project in Newcastle (NCC, 2002). As this study was completed before the introduction of the pilot, it can offer only limited indications of the possible impact of choice-based lettings on 16- and 17-year-olds who are accepted as statutorily homeless. A large majority of the sample, 119 or 82.1%, were rehoused within three months of the original homelessness application. This raises a question as to whether, under the choice-based scheme, the remainder would either have lost their priority for housing or been forced to accept property in an area that they did not want.

There are clearly some difficult judgments to be made as to whether it is more desirable to offer choice to homeless households or to rehouse them quickly, particularly if they are staying in temporary accommodation and imposing costs on the local authority. This dilemma is likely to be particularly acute in areas with a smaller supply of vacancies than Newcastle, where approximately 4,000 properties are allocated each year (personal communication with a member of the Community and Housing Directorate, 14 March 2003). This research suggests that allowing young homeless people the time to choose a property close to their support networks is likely to have long-term benefits in terms of successful tenancies.

The advantage of providing a choice of area was most starkly illustrated by the greater incidence of successful tenancies among those young people who became local authority or In Line tenants, compared to those who were rehoused into projects located at fixed sites. The difficulties caused by geographically defined projects was demonstrated further when, after the period of the study, housing management problems at Gill Street led to support services being withdrawn: the block is no longer available as supported accommodation for young people (personal communication with a member of the Community and Housing Directorate, 15 July 2003).

The research could not determine whether forms of support linked to specific buildings would carry the same disadvantages in an area with higher overall demand for housing and a lower supply of vacancies. In such an area most young people might find that they could not be rehoused into a location of their preference, regardless of the type of accommodation that they were allocated. However, the failure of nine of the ten sample members who were rehoused into projects on fixed sites suggests that all housing providers should re-examine the effectiveness of this type of provision for young people and consider whether 'floating' forms of support might be more effective.

Education, training and benefits

In addition to its efforts to bring about neighbourhood renewal, the government has sought to tackle social exclusion at the level of the individual by providing access to work, education and training for a variety of groups, including young people and homeless people. The sample were less likely to be involved in these activities than other people in the same age group. The Office of the Deputy Prime Minister (ODPM, 2001) has suggested that 'economic' activity can help to prevent tenancy breakdown, by reducing the incidence of debt and isolation. However, the surprising failure in tenancies of the small number of female sample members who were receiving a training allowance or studying for GCSEs suggests that this belief is mistaken.

Instead, the beneficial effect of advice workers helping young people to access benefits suggests that the government should reconsider the role that benefits can play in enabling young people to make a success of their first independent tenancy. A time-limited entitlement to means-tested benefit for those 16- and 17-year-olds who are forced to live independently could provide a valuable breathing space from regular daytime activity and enable the young person to concentrate on the new responsibilities of managing their own home.

There would clearly be difficulties associated with restoring an entitlement to benefits for this group. Such a measure would not address the risk of social exclusion in the longer term, whatever the short-term benefits in terms of conducting a successful tenancy. For a government keen to balance rights and responsibilities, there would also be an ideological difficulty with a young person receiving financial support yet not being required to undertake any form of 'productive' activity in return. The present government has not expressed the same fears as its Conservative predecessors about providing 'perverse incentives' for young people to leave their parents' home unnecessarily, but there would be a substantial political risk in creating a situation where 16- and 17-year-olds living independently had an entitlement to benefits but those who continued to live with their parent(s) did not.

There are a number of points that can be made to allay such concerns. The government has expressed a commitment to create a "learning society" (see, for example, DfES, 2001) and its skills strategy White Paper (DfES, 2003, pp 24-5) proposed measures to provide adults who lack formal qualifications with opportunities to study. If these opportunities are to be genuinely available to all, then a time-limited break from education and training should be retrievable at a later stage. Concerns that providing an entitlement to means-tested benefit before the age of 18 creates an imbalance between rights and responsibilities could be dealt with by introducing extra regulations for young people who exercise this entitlement, meaning that they would need to continue in work, education or training – rather than claim means-tested benefit again – until some time after their eighteenth birthday. The argument that providing an entitlement to benefits would lead to young people leaving home unnecessarily is similar to the frequently advanced one that young, single women are encouraged to become pregnant by the availability of benefits and council housing. However, research among teenage mothers has suggested that few were aware of the availability of these services at the point when they became pregnant (Allen and Dowling, 1998, pp 101, 105-6). In addition, any possible incentive effect could be countered by making greater efforts to inform young people about the difficulties involved in living independently – a point that is returned to later in this chapter.

The tendency of young women to fail in their tenancies if involved in education or training, together with the high failure rate of sample members rehoused into projects at fixed locations, has implications for two other areas of government policy. The first of these is the support given to foyers. Young people moving into a foyer building do not have a choice about where to live and so may become isolated from their social support networks[1]. In addition, while the approach of seeking to solve young people's housing and employment difficulties may be regarded as holistic, this research suggests that it would be more helpful for a young person to find housing first and then to consider employment, training and educational opportunities once they have had some time to settle into their own tenancy. Evaluations of foyers (for example, Quilgars and Anderson, 1995) have tended to concentrate on the immediate outcomes – particularly the numbers of young people who leave having found both work and housing. A longitudinal study is needed, comparing the eventual housing situation of former foyer residents with that of young people rehoused into independent tenancies, in order to determine whether the concerns raised by this research are reflected in poorer long-term prospects for former foyer residents.

The research findings also question the effectiveness of some of the government's policies for young parents, which include help to continue in education (SEU, 1999b, p 107) and providing some form of supported accommodation for those who cannot live with parents or a partner (SEU, 1999b, p 102). Government guidance suggests that the supported accommodation can be in the form of floating support schemes. However, the guidance also identifies three options linking support to specific buildings: hostels, self-contained flats with access to communal areas and cooperative communities (where residents share meals and household tasks) (DTLR and Teenage Pregnancy Unit, 2001, pp 7-9).

In addition to the research findings concerning building-based services and the impact of continuing in education, there are other reasons for suggesting that these policies are inappropriate. The government claims that there is a consensus among young mothers that childcare should be an important element of any supported living arrangement (DTLR and Teenage Pregnancy Unit, 2001, pp 10-11). However, this is not consistent with the findings of a follow-up to the main study described in this book (discussed further later in this chapter). In the follow-up study, when 17 respondents who had dependent children were asked whether they would prefer accommodation where help with childcare was provided, none responded positively. In addition, unpublished, qualitative research into the housing needs and aspirations of young lone parents (Harding and Kirk, 2002) revealed little enthusiasm for any housing option other than self-contained accommodation. A key reason for this preference was that the respondents wanted to be rehoused close to their informal support networks of family and friends.

Finally, the research suggested that lone parents are the wrong group of young people for the government to devote special attention to. Although the number of respondents with dependent children was too small to reveal many statistically significant differences with the remainder of the sample, those differences that were found suggested a relatively positive experience of independent living. Rather than focusing on lone parents, the government should consider methods of providing extra support to those overlapping groups of young people who were particularly likely to experience difficulties living in their own housing: young men, people who stayed in local authority temporary accommodation and those who had experienced high numbers of social problems.

The need for strategies and an evidence base

In addition to a commitment to tackling social exclusion, a key element of government policy that is relevant to this study is the requirement for local authorities to plan strategically and to provide evidence to demonstrate the benefits of services.

The data demonstrated that there were links between the outcome of a tenancy, the informal support that was available and the level of social problems in the immediate area. These findings suggest that the needs of young people living independently will only be met effectively if there is integration between strategies in the three key areas of regeneration, Supporting People and homelessness.

At another level, the requirements to create homelessness and Supporting People strategies are an opportunity to specify the types of support service that should be provided to young people and other vulnerable groups. In an era of stringent performance measurement, authorities need to be consistently collecting and updating data with which to evaluate these services.

One key issue to consider in any evaluation is how the impact of services will be measured. Local authorities have powers to develop their own Supporting People performance indicators, in addition to those specified by central government. The research described in this book provides one possible method of measuring success and failure of young people's tenancies, based on tenancy length, reason for termination of tenancy and repeat homelessness applications. There were criticisms of this method, with some workers arguing that young people who terminated their tenancies quickly for positive reasons – such as a successful reconciliation with parents – should not be judged to have failed. However, the approach used seemed more sensitive than simply concentrating on length of tenancy (or tenancy sustainment), as much previous work has done.

The development of more sophisticated measures to monitor the impact of services is likely to require a substantial investment of staff time to collect the necessary information. However, it is clearly in the interests of local authorities and other organisations to collate the data that are needed to establish the effectiveness of services: the allocation of Supporting People grants gives authorities a lever with which to ensure that all organisations take this responsibility seriously.

One example of an attempt to build an evidence base of services provided and their impact is a new method of data collection initiated by Newcastle City Council since the completion of the original research. This system is used in the case of all people under the age of 21 accepted as statutorily homeless, although in practice the vast majority of people in this category are 16- or 17-year-olds. A young person who approaches the local authority as homeless is asked to sign a consent form, saying that they are willing for information to be shared between agencies and with a researcher. This ensures that they are not asked the same question twice, but also provides the opportunity for a progressively more detailed record to be compiled of their circumstances and views, and the services with which they are provided. The stages of data collection are as follows:

Stage 1   the assessment of the homelessness application.
Stage 2   an assessment of support needs conducted by a worker from the voluntary sector (usually the NIN or In Line).
Stage 3   a record of advice and support received while the young person stays in temporary accommodation.
Stage 4   a record of the support received in the first six months of tenancy, compiled by the worker most involved in providing long-term support.
Stage 5   a record of the outcome of the tenancy, completed one year from the tenancy start date. The homelessness section collects the information that is necessary to evaluate tenancies according to similar definitions of 'success' and 'failure' to the ones used in the original research.

A slightly different system has been created in the case of care leavers.

This system of data collection requires a substantial commitment from workers of all the agencies involved and administrative systems that can facilitate the passing of records from stage to stage efficiently. There were some initial difficulties in ensuring that the information collected about each young person was comprehensive, with lower than expected returns at some stages of the process and several examples of unanswered questions on forms. After approximately fourteen months of the new system, 352 Stage 1 assessments had been completed and, in relation to these 352, there were 217 completed Stage 2 forms, 24 Stage 3 forms (22 of them in relation to young people who had stayed at Hill Court) and 37 Stage 4 forms.

No Stage 5 assessments had been completed, largely because of the timescale involved; the small number of Stage 4 forms was also partly due to the requirement to complete this form six months from the tenancy start date. The low number of Stage 3 forms reflected to some extent the limited number of young people who stayed in temporary accommodation. There were undoubtedly difficulties in creating comprehensive records, but the data collected have provided evidence with which to make a further evaluation of services provided in Newcastle. This is referred to in this chapter as the follow-up study.

Implications of findings for specific services

The data from both the original research and the follow-up study provided evidence of the type of support services that are likely to have the most beneficial effects on young people's tenancy outcomes. It seems likely that, if replicated elsewhere, these services would increase the number of 16- and 17-year-olds succeeding in tenancies.

Material forms of support

It has already been noted that the original study suggested that it was important to help young people to claim benefits but could show few other positive effects of services to meet material needs, beyond short-term tenant satisfaction. The high incidence of debt among the sample, despite the range of agencies offering financial advice, was a matter for particular concern. As the second interviews suggested that debts were increasingly likely to be owed to the local authority, it seems likely that finding more effective methods of meeting material needs would serve the interests of both young tenants and their landlords.

It is possible, of course, that the incidence of debt simply indicated that young people's income was inadequate to meet their day-to-day needs. However, the findings demonstrated that, with the exception of staying in local authority temporary accommodation, the variables with the greatest influence over whether a respondent was in debt at the first interview were those related to consumption of alcohol, cigarettes and drugs. Of the 74 first interview respondents who smoked, 45 (60.8%) said that they wanted to reduce the number of cigarettes they consumed: a similar figure to the seven out of ten smokers of all ages that the government believes wish to give up (DoH, 2003a). This finding points to a slightly different approach for support workers, although they may feel that helping young people to overcome addictions is not part of the role that they have been trained for or that they aspire to. However, another option is to refer young people to the smoking cessation services that have been established in every health authority (DoH, 2003b). This may have a greater effect than more conventional support services such as providing budgeting advice.

A slightly different picture emerged when considering the characteristics of respondents who had fallen into debt by the time of the second interview. They were particularly likely to say that they had experienced unexpected problems in independent living, which suggests that they might have benefited from warnings about the cost of living in their own property. Such information could be provided to young tenants alongside advice about tenancy conditions and rent obligations, in an attempt to ensure that a realistic view is taken.

One form of material support provided in Newcastle, where there is already a considerable body of evidence to show housing management benefits, is the provision of part-furnished tenancies. The original study could not add to this evidence when considering the sample as a whole, but could demonstrate that being allocated part-furnished accommodation had a positive impact on the tenancy outcomes of lone parents. It should be noted that Newcastle City Council has taken steps to deal with some of the concerns that the sample expressed about the furniture package. At the time of writing, it is preparing to introduce a menu system for part-furnished tenancies, with tenants able to choose different items of furniture from a range of options. Among the new items that can be selected are those that respondents were particularly likely to complain that they were lacking: cookers, fridges and settees. Carpets are still only provided in fully furnished accommodation, as the furniture package is intended to be re-usable. However, a large living room rug is one of the items that can be chosen from the menu (personal communication with a member of the Community and Housing Directorate, 18 June 2003).

Preparing young people for difficulties

The finding that sample members who had fallen into debt by the time of the second interview were more likely to say that they had experienced unexpected problems was one of a number that suggested there was a risk of young people being unprepared for independent living and taking an unduly optimistic view. The government has used two approaches to tackle this risk. The first is to seek to dissuade young people from leaving home 'prematurely'; the second is to provide those who do leave with advice about the difficulties involved in living independently. Education and family mediation services have been identified as important elements of the first approach. However, the research suggested that further consideration needs to be given to the method of providing both these services if they are to be effective.

Previous studies (see, for example, Jones, 1995, p 150; Harding, 1997, pp 3-4) have suggested that one difficulty with providing leaving home education in schools is that the young people who are most likely to need the information are least likely to be there. The finding that over half the first interview respondents had not regularly attended school confirms this view. It suggests that education in schools needs to be supplemented by more innovative approaches to providing information to those young people who are hardest to reach with conventional services.

The follow-up study suggested that providing family mediation services at the point of a homelessness application is unlikely to facilitate a return home. Of the 217 young people whose three self-identified main support needs were recorded on the Stage 2 form, only one chose the family mediation option. Similarly, only two of the 187 who specified their preferred form of housing and support said that they would like to return to their parents or carers. In contrast, a study of adolescent support teams (Biehal et al, 2000) suggested that preventative work at an earlier stage can prevent homelessness by helping young people to leave home in a planned manner. It appears that mediation services are likely to be ineffective at the stage of a young person presenting themselves as homeless, and instead should concentrate on those whose relationship with their parents has not yet reached the point of breaking down.

For young people who cannot be prevented from leaving home, the government has sought to tackle unrealistic expectations by encouraging a 'reality check' to ensure that they understand the difficulties associated with finding and keeping accommodation (DTLR, 2002b, p 47). The research suggested that such an approach is appropriate: providing advice about tenancy conditions and/or rent obligations at the start of a tenancy was shown by the original study to be an effective means of increasing the likelihood of success.

Providing services perceived to be less important

The original study revealed a discrepancy between the forms of support that were reported and valued by young people and those that were shown to have a positive effect on tenancy outcomes. Despite its beneficial effect, there was little acknowledgement among the sample that advice about tenancy conditions or rent obligations was necessary. In contrast, the young people seemed to particularly value material forms of support, even though this support had a limited impact on tenancy outcome.

This picture was reinforced in the follow-up study by the response that young people gave to the questions asking them to identify their support needs. The frequency with which different forms of support were chosen is shown in Table 5.1.

Despite the limited number of young people acknowledging a need for advice about tenancy conditions or rent obligations, the Stage 4 reports (which recorded support provided in the first six months of the tenancy) suggested that workers had been able to provide such advice in the majority of cases. Of the 37 reports that were received, in 24 cases (64.9%) young people were provided with advice or assistance about tenancy conditions and there were also 24 cases where advice or assistance about making rent payments was given.

Table 5.1: Support needs identified by young people at Stage 2 assessment

Type of support	Number
Benefits advice	114
Social Fund or charity applications	113
Furnishing accommodation	81
Tenancy set up	60
Advocacy	54
Assistance with fuel connection/payments	41
Advice (type unspecified)	27
Advice about tenancy conditions	26
Advice about rent obligations	17
Assistance with safety and security	13
Advice about employment	8
Advice about training	8
Counselling/emotional support	8
Advice about debt	7
Assistance with life skills	7
Advice about relationships	3
Support over mental health issues	2
Other	17

There were similar findings when considering advice about being assertive with friends. The original study had suggested that this form of support would be beneficial because those young people who said that they could not control visitors to their property all failed in their tenancy. A specific question at Stage 2 of the follow-up study was answered by 187 young people, with only 35 (18.7%) saying that they needed advice about how to be assertive. However, 17 of the 37 Stage 4 records (45.9%) showed that advice about this subject had been provided.

Giving young people advice that they do not perceive to be necessary may seem inconsistent with philosophies that value empowering, client-centred services. However, if services are to continue to be provided, they must be able to demonstrate that they provide benefits to the landlord. It seems crucial that advice workers, while not ignoring the expressed wishes of young people, concentrate on those forms of advice and assistance that have been shown to have a positive effect on tenancy outcomes.

Acknowledging diversity and reaching the most disadvantaged young people

A key finding to emerge from the original study was the existence of extensive differences in the circumstances, views and needs of young men and young women. Young women were particularly likely to be hindered by overconfidence and seemed most likely to benefit from the type of 'cautionary' advice discussed earlier. In contrast, young men were likely to lack confidence about independent living and to benefit from intensive support and/or a feeling that they had been adequately advised.

The need of young men for ongoing support was further emphasised by the follow-up study, which suggested that they were less likely than young women to be involved with an agency at the time of their homelessness application ($p<0.001$) (see Table 5.2).

The apparent need to concentrate longer-term support on young men raises a difficult issue for service providers: to provide young women mainly with one-off advice about tenancy conditions, rent obligations and being assertive with friends, while increasing the access of young men to ongoing support, naturally raises issues about discrimination on the grounds of gender. However, the data suggested that this approach can be justified by reference to gender

Table 5.2: Cross table of whether involved with other professional by gender: follow-up study

		Gender			
		Male	**Female**	**Couple**	**Total**
Involved with other professional?	Yes	1	38	1	**40**
	No	46	69	0	**115**
Total		47	107	1	155

differences in the types of service that have a beneficial effect on tenancy outcomes.

As has been noted previously, young men were only one of a number of overlapping groups that the original study suggested were particularly likely to experience tenancy failure. In the case of two others – those who stayed in local authority temporary accommodation and those with substantial experience of social problems – there were particular difficulties with low take up of some services.

The lack of reported use of the extensive support available at Hill Court was one particularly disappointing finding of the original study. The response of the local authority was to introduce an appointments system to ensure that everyone admitted to Hill Court met with an Advice and Support Worker (ASW: a new support team that incorporated the SPAT workers). The follow-up study suggested that this measure may have ensured that more young people were helped to access a regular source of benefit income. Of the 22 cases where a Stage 3 form was completed, 11 young people had entered Hill Court with no income. By the time that they left, four of these 11 were having a claim for benefit dealt with and three were known to have a regular income.

However, there appeared to be continuing low take up of other services. Of the 22 young people:

• four had been given advice about fuel connections or payments but two had refused this advice;
• four had been given advice about tenancy conditions but three had refused;
• six had been given advice about rent payments but four had refused; and
• all five who had been offered advice about how to cook, clean and shop had refused.

The continuing difficulties in providing services to the particularly disadvantaged group of young people who stay in temporary accommodation is one particularly problematic finding of this research. It remains to be seen whether an innovative method of increasing take up of services among this group can be found.

Whatever the difficulties of targeting services on young men, or on young people who stay in local authority temporary accommodation, they are, at least, two easily identifiable groups. There may be even greater problems for local authorities and other agencies in trying to concentrate services on young people with high numbers of social problems, as they are a group that cannot easily be identified. It seems highly unlikely that legal restrictions on the sharing of data between organisations would allow housing departments to collect information about involvement in crime from criminal justice agencies, or attendance at school from the education department. Instead, it seems that this information could only be collected by direct questioning of young people.

However, agencies conducting the Stage 2 assessment in the follow-up study argued that asking questions about sensitive subjects such as these would hinder the process of building a trusting relationship with a young person. Their refusal to ask these questions appeared to be justified when examining the positive relationships that were developed through the Stage 2 assessments, as will be discussed further later in this chapter.

So local authorities and other agencies face a seemingly impossible task if they wish to identify at an early stage those young people who have had a high level of involvement in social problems. Perhaps the only method of increasing take up of services by this group is to ensure greater service use by young men and people who stay in local authority temporary accommodation – although this, too, has been shown to be problematic.

Reaching all young people with services

While there appeared to be ongoing problems in reaching the most disadvantaged groups with services, the follow-up study provided more positive findings in terms of increasing service take up among young people as a whole. As a result of the evidence provided by the original study of low take up of services, the local authority, the NIN and In Line agreed to a more proactive method of providing support. Rather than a homelessness officer making a referral for a young person to go to visit a support agency, it was decided that a worker from the NIN and/or In Line would be based in the homelessness section every afternoon, which is the time of day when young people are interviewed. Once a homelessness officer had completed their assessment, a young person would be offered a Stage 2 assessment of their support needs without having to leave the building.

This type of approach seems consistent with much current thinking about good practice in providing services to homeless people. Central government has praised joint assessments of housing and support needs (for example, Audit Commission, 2003, p 20), particularly services such as the Hub in Bristol, where help, advice and information are provided to single people in housing need from one location (ODPM, 2001, p 10).

The evidence of the follow-up study suggested that this praise is deserved and that providing homelessness and support needs assessments from the same building has had a positive impact in Newcastle. Workers reported a closer relationship between the statutory and voluntary sectors as a result of this change but the key benefit appeared to be a greater take up of support services. It was noted earlier that 217 of the 352 young people assessed at Stage 1 (61.6%) were also known to have received a Stage 2 assessment. Although this figure is likely to be an underestimate due to initial difficulties in collating records, it still represents a substantial improvement on the 36.6% who were assessed by SNAP in the original study.

One benefit of the greater number of assessments of support needs was that young people, having made contact with a support worker, often seemed eager for that contact to continue. This was demonstrated by the responses to a question on the Stage 2 assessment asking which form of housing and support

Table 5.3: Cross table of requested type of housing and support by agency of Stage 2 worker: follow-up study

		Agency of Stage 2 worker			
		NIN	**LCST**	**In Line**	**Total**
Young person's	In Line	19	2	38	**59**
requested	NIN	89	0	3	**92**
type	NIN or supported housing	6	0	0	**6**
of housing/	Supported housing	6	0	0	**6**
support	Stepping Stones	1	0	0	**1**
	No support	18	2	1	**21**
	Return to live with family/carers	2	0	0	**2**
Total		141	4	42	187

a young person would prefer. In a large majority of cases, they expressed a wish to be supported by the agency of the worker who was conducting the assessment ($p=0.01$) (see Table 5.3).

These findings support the claim of the Office of the Deputy Prime Minister (2003e) that:

> The initial contact with a service is very important to young people. They like services where it is easy to walk in, the atmosphere is warm and the staff are welcoming.

While the willingness of young people to engage with an agency after meeting one of its workers seems a very positive finding, one possible negative perspective is that the choice of key support agency was influenced more by the random allocation of the worker for the Stage 2 interview than by the needs of the young person. This may have been a less significant issue than in the past because, by the time of the follow-up study, the NIN had formed a One to One team, which conducted most of the Stage 2 assessments and which offered support that could be as intense as that of In Line, (although without the housing management function). However, analysis of the Stage 4 forms showed that some differences persisted in the types of support provided: for example, In Line tenants were particularly likely to be offered help with cooking ($p=0.057$), cleaning ($p=0.055$) and shopping ($p=<0.001$).

Summary

When summarising the practical implications of the research findings, it may be helpful to separate the key points relating to central government policy from those concerning the approach of local authorities. In the case of central government, the most important implications are as follows:

- The concept of social exclusion is helpful to an understanding of the broad range of disadvantages that are faced by many young people living independently.
- It is also helpful and appropriate that the government takes a broad view of neighbourhood renewal: measures that can tackle crime and antisocial behaviour seem particularly likely to benefit young people who have their own tenancy.
- However, the government's favoured method of tackling social exclusion at the individual level – facilitating education and training – seems unhelpful for 16- and 17-year-olds who are living independently. An entitlement to claim benefits, if only for a short period at the beginning of a tenancy, could increase the likelihood of a successful outcome.
- In addition to the findings in the area of education and training, the failure of the young people who were rehoused into projects at fixed locations suggests that the government should reconsider both its support for foyers and its approach to young lone parents who are living independently.
- In seeking to discourage young people from leaving home unnecessarily, the government should look for alternative locations to schools for providing education about housing and homelessness. It should also encourage the provision of mediation services that work with families before a young person becomes homeless.

For local authorities, key implications of the research findings for the services that they provide themselves, or facilitate through other organisations, are:

- While it can be difficult to persuade young people to access services that are available, these difficulties can be eased by locating support workers in the building where homelessness assessments take place.
- There remains a need to find methods by which the particularly disadvantaged group of young people who stay in local authority temporary accommodation can be encouraged to access services.
- Gender differences should be acknowledged in the provision of support services, with an emphasis on providing information to young women at an early stage about the difficulties that are involved in independent living, while giving more ongoing support and advice to young men.
- It is both desirable and feasible to provide young people – especially young women – with advice about independent living that they may not perceive to be important: specifically, advice about rent obligations, tenancy conditions and being assertive with friends.
- There is a need to continue to provide the types of material assistance that have been shown to improve tenancy outcomes – namely, helping young people to access benefits and providing part-furnished accommodation. In addition to these services, the most effective means of improving young people's financial position may be to warn them at an early stage about the

difficulties that they face and to offer them support to reduce spending on cigarettes, drugs and alcohol.

• Every effort should be made to rehouse young people close to their sources of informal support. Where choice-based lettings systems are introduced, their impact on the ability of homeless people to be rehoused into their neighbourhood of choice should be evaluated.

• In regeneration work, there is a need to ensure that, wherever possible, demolition of property does not entail breaking up young people's support networks.

Findings about the effects of different services and policy approaches have a bearing on explanations of the difficulties that young people face in independent living. The final chapter will re-examine these explanations in the light of the research findings.

Note

[1] This concern does not, of course, apply to 'dispersed' foyers, but to traditional foyer developments, where accommodation, support and job search facilities are provided on one site.

SIX

Young people in independent tenancies: what is the problem?

This chapter uses the data from the original study to evaluate the three explanations for young people experiencing difficulties in independent tenancies that were discussed in Chapter One. The key difficulty considered is tenancy failure, but there is also consideration of a number of other long-term problems that were revealed by responses to second interview questions. These problems are being in trouble with the police in the early months of a tenancy, falling into debt for the first time, reduced optimism about independent living and experiencing a worsening relationship with parents.

Failings on the part of the individual

The effect of involvement in social problems

It was noted in Chapter One that explanations of difficulties that are based on young people's personal characteristics tend not to emphasise any antisocial or 'deviant' behaviour on their part, but instead take the less critical approach of focusing on their inexperience or immaturity. However, it was impossible to thoroughly examine the data without considering the effect of young people's experience of social problems – or, to take a less generous view, the extent to which they had been involved in problematic behaviour.

The findings left little doubt that 16- and 17-year-olds rehoused as homeless in Newcastle are more likely than other people of the same age to have experienced difficulties such as absence from school or trouble with the police. There was also clear evidence of a concentration of these problems among some members of the sample. The effect of these problems on long-term difficulties was quite substantial. Drug taking at the first interview increased the risk that a respondent's relationship with their parents would have deteriorated by the time of the second, as did high scores on the index of social problems. High scores on the index were also associated with worsening feelings about independent living and failure in tenancies.

The effect of the number of social problems on tenancy outcomes was also evident when considering young men separately. Similarly, accepting a tenancy with In Line increased the likelihood of tenancy success for both the sample as a whole and young men in particular. Although the intense support provided by In Line is intended to meet a range of needs, the original reason for the local authority's support for the organisation was concerns over some young people's "significant behavioural problems" (NCC, 1997). So a measure aimed specifically at problematic behaviour appears to have reduced the incidence of tenancy failure.

However, the number of social problems had no statistically significant effect on the tenancy outcomes of female sample members, suggesting that it is among young men that the experience of such problems is most closely linked to long-term difficulties.

The young person as inexperienced

The research also provided some evidence to support a view that long-term difficulties are a result of inexperience or immaturity on the part of young people. These ideas are often linked to the idea that assistance is needed with budgeting and/or 'life skills'. The need for better money management was demonstrated by debt at the first interview being linked to spending patterns rather than level of income or other material circumstances. When considering the longer-term problem of debts being acquired between the interviews, there was evidence to suggest that young people were particularly at risk if they had not anticipated difficulties arising. These findings suggest that financial problems are at least partly a result of young people's inexperience.

When taking a narrow interpretation of 'life skills' as domestic skills, the data linking the level of these skills to long-term problems were ambiguous, with the young people who rated their abilities as particularly high or particularly low being more likely to fail in their tenancies. However, if the 'life skills' term is given a broader definition of taking a realistic and informed approach to independent living, it is a particularly helpful concept for understanding young people's long-term difficulties. The striking decline in confidence between the first and the second interviews may be regarded as evidence that many young people initially had unrealistic expectations. This view is supported by the finding that sample members who were willing to acknowledge difficulties at an early stage were less likely to subsequently report deteriorating feelings about independent living.

There was also evidence to suggest that an initially negative (or realistic) view could have a beneficial effect in terms of tenancy outcomes, particularly for young women. The implication that avoiding overconfidence and naivety can increase the likelihood of success was reinforced by the positive effect – for young women in particular, in addition to the sample as a whole – of support workers providing information about the legal obligations of tenants.

A different set of factors suggested that the difficulties that young men experienced in their own tenancies were due to their inexperience or immaturity. They were more likely than the young women to expect problems in independent living and were particularly likely to fail in their tenancies if they felt that they did not have enough advice. The benefit that they appeared to derive from contact with support services implied that a feeling of being well supported and advised improved the likelihood of tenancy success. A more critical interpretation of these findings is to cite Campbell's (1993, pp 202-3) view that young men want someone to look after them.

It may seem disingenuous to argue that young men need to feel supported in independent living, and young women need to feel less confident, and then to interpret both these findings as indicating that difficulties and failure in tenancies are caused by immaturity or inexperience. However, both factors point to the need to adopt a realistic and informed approach. They also suggest that an independent tenancy is a responsibility that some young people are not yet prepared for, with support needed to make good the shortfall in their preparations.

Structural failings

Financial hardship

The research demonstrated that many young people living in their own tenancies suffer sustained material hardship but provided relatively few examples of this hardship increasing the risk of experiencing other long-term problems such as tenancy failure. For example, 45 of the 94 first interview respondents (47.9%) said that their accommodation was inadequately furnished. However, lack of furniture was linked to long-term difficulties in only one instance: lone parents were more likely to fail in their tenancies if their accommodation was unfurnished. Indeed, there was one finding to suggest that shortage of furniture could have a positive effect: young people were less likely to experience deteriorating feelings about independent living if they considered their accommodation to be inadequately furnished at the first interview.

A similar pattern emerged with regard to financial hardship. The sample tended to have low incomes and to rate their money situation poorly, with large numbers regularly borrowing money and finding that their money did not last until the end of the week. However, there were only two instances where these circumstances were linked to long-term difficulties: respondents who rated their financial situation poorly at the first interview were more likely to have been in trouble with the police by the time of the second, and those first interview respondents who had no income were particularly likely to experience tenancy failure.

In two other cases there was a slightly surprising relationship between material factors and long-term difficulties. Respondents who said, at the first interview, that they did not yet know whether their money would last until the end of the week (most of whom were awaiting benefit payments) were particularly likely to conduct successful tenancies. Similarly, young women who had no income at their first contact with advice workers (rather than at the first interview) were also particularly likely to succeed. Both these findings suggested that receiving benefits after an initial delay has a positive effect on tenancy outcomes. This is consistent with the other evidence that suggests that initial difficulties in independent living can have a beneficial effect by encouraging a more realistic view.

Residualisation

While the research could provide only limited evidence of links between material hardship and long-term difficulties, it demonstrated clearly that a young person's opinion of the area they were living in affected the likelihood that their tenancy would be successful. This finding supports the view expressed in other work (Hutson, 1999, pp 214-15; Fitzpatrick, 2000, p 36) that a positive view of the area is very important to young people who are living independently. The most common reason given for disliking an area – or terminating a tenancy – was the experience or fear of crime and antisocial behaviour. This difficulty was not restricted to hard-to-let areas, suggesting that the most helpful concept for explaining area-based problems is residualisation, particularly the idea that the concentration of disadvantaged households in local authority housing has contributed to a widespread process of neighbourhood decline.

Failings in informal support

The reasons that most sample members gave for liking the area that they were living in focused on the availability of informal support. The value that they placed on advice about independent living from informal sources also showed the importance that they attached to relationships with family and friends. However, relationships with friends appeared to have a much greater impact on the likelihood of experiencing long-term difficulties than family relationships.

The role of family

Most first interview respondents viewed their family relationships positively and most saw their parents either daily or weekly. The evidence that over half the second interview respondents felt that their relationship with their parents had improved confirms the findings of Jones (1995, p 90) and Fitzpatrick (2000, p 91) that leaving home can improve the relationship with parents. The research could offer no support to the view (expressed, for example, by Smith et al, 1998, p 38) that men living independently may find it particularly difficult to maintain relationships with their family. The idea that young people from lone-parent families are particularly likely to experience poor family relationships (Murray, 1990, 1994; Dennis and Erdos, 1993) also found no support from the research, except in the case of the minority who stayed in local authority temporary accommodation.

Care leavers were an important group to study when considering the effect of family relationships because it was assumed that they had experienced either the death of parents or a complete breakdown in relationships at some point in the past. Shortcomings in the informal support available to them were evident from them being particularly unlikely to say that their family and friends were a good help. Care leavers were overrepresented in the sample, but not to the same extent as has been observed in studies of homeless people in other geographical areas. This was one of a number of indicators that support services can go some way towards overcoming the lack of family support available. Another was that, although they were more likely to have high numbers of social problems than other sample members, care leavers did not face a higher risk of experiencing any long-term problems.

The small minority of second interview respondents who reported that their relationship with their parents had deteriorated were likely to experience increasing difficulties in a number of areas. However, the research could provide only one example of a clear causal relationship between family difficulties and long-term problems: respondents who said that they did not get on well with their family at the first interview were more likely to subsequently be in trouble with the police. This study suggests that family relationships are not key influences on young people's experience of independent living.

The role of friends

The sample also tended to report a positive relationship with their peer group, with 83 first interview respondents (88.3%) saying that they had quite a few friends. However, the minority who experienced problems in this area were more likely to face long-term difficulties. This was evident from the higher rate of tenancy failure among the group of respondents who stayed in local authority temporary accommodation, who were assumed to be socially isolated and were particularly unlikely to say that they had quite a few friends.

Among the sample as a whole, staying in local authority temporary accommodation was one of the four variables with the greatest influence on tenancy outcomes. The other three – whether a respondent had quite a few friends, whether they could control visitors to their property and whether they had ever tried drugs – all appeared to be linked to peer group relationships. A small minority of young women reported that they were unable to control visitors to their property – all failed in their tenancy. In contrast, experience of drug taking (which may also be a reflection of an unhelpful peer group) particularly affected the likelihood of young men conducting a successful tenancy.

The only finding regarding friends that was not consistent with this picture was that first interview respondents who said that they did not have quite a few friends were less likely than other sample members to subsequently experience deteriorating feelings about independent living. However, the balance of the evidence clearly demonstrates that a supportive peer group is of substantial benefit to a 16- or 17-year-old who has their own tenancy.

Gender differences

The discussion earlier in this chapter highlights the different factors affecting the tenancy outcomes of young men and young women. Indeed, there was no variable that had a statistically significant effect on the likelihood of success among both groups. It was not possible to make comparisons in relation to other long-term difficulties because only three young men were interviewed at the second stage, making it very unlikely that significant relationships would be found between gender and second interview variables.

Gender itself was highly placed on the list of variables that had the greatest effect on tenancy outcomes, with young men being particularly likely to fail. This was perhaps unsurprising given the wide range of disadvantages that they suffered, including lower incomes, a less favourable view of their own health and a higher level of experience of social problems.

There was a substantial overlap between young men and respondents who had stayed in local authority temporary accommodation: 11 of the 12 sample members who fell into both these categories failed in their tenancies. Among both groups, tenancy failure was more likely if they felt insufficiently advised about independent living. So being male, suffering from social isolation and feeling poorly prepared seem to be a particularly disadvantageous set of characteristics when beginning an independent tenancy.

Summary

The findings in relation to young men show that explanations of young people's difficulties in independent living cannot be viewed in isolation from each other: a combination of personal characteristics and lack of social support contributed to a greater risk of tenancy failure. The links between the explanations were further illustrated by considering some of the relationships between first interview variables and long-term difficulties:

• Drug taking at the time of the first interview increased the risk of a young person's relationship with their parents subsequently deteriorating.
• Respondents who did not get on well with their family at the time of the first interview were particularly likely to be in trouble with the police between the interviews.
• First interview respondents who rated their money situation poorly were also more likely to subsequently be in trouble with the police.
• First interview respondents who did not expect problems in independent living were particularly likely to fall into debt by the time of the second interview.

In addition to a failure to acknowledge links between different explanations of young people's difficulties in independent tenancies, one major weakness of current thinking is that it gives insufficient consideration to the role of gender differences. When considering modifications that should be made to each of the three explanations in the light of the research findings, gender is a feature in every case. The modifications are as follows:

- When considering the role of individual factors, concern about problematic behaviour should focus on young men. It should also be noted that characteristics that can be seen as immature affect young people's experiences in different ways: young women tend to be disadvantaged if they are overconfident while young men are adversely affected by a feeling that they are inadequately advised.
- Existing discussions of the role of material factors correctly identify the importance of young people liking the area that they are living in and feeling safe from crime and antisocial behaviour. However, at the individual level, the role of material hardships has been overemphasised – among young women some initial financial difficulties may even have a positive effect.
- In discussions of the informal support available to young people, there has been too much concentration on the role of the family. Although the specific factors involved vary between young men and young women, the likelihood of conducting a successful tenancy is substantially increased by positive and supportive relationships with friends.

These points should be incorporated into current thinking about young people's difficulties in independent living and translated into more appropriate service provision. The result is likely to be a greater number of successful tenancies and more 16- and 17-year-olds enjoying the full benefit of the 2002 changes to the homelessness legislation.

References

Ainley, P. (1991) *Young people leaving home*, London: Cassell Education Limited.

Alcock, P. (1994) 'Welfare rights and wrongs: The limits of anti-poverty strategies', *Local Government Studies*, vol 9, no 2, pp 134-52.

Allen, I. and Dowling, S. B. (1998) *Teenage mothers*, London: Policy Studies Institute.

AMA (Association of Metropolitan Authorities) (1994) *Preparing for CCT: Specifying housing management*, London: AMA.

Anderson, I., Kemp, P. and Quilgars, D. (1993) *Single homeless people*, London: DoE.

Andrews, K. and Jacobs, J. (1990) *Punishing the poor*, Basingstoke: Macmillan.

Ashton, D., Maguire, M. and Spilsbury, M. (1990) *Restructuring the labour market*, Basingstoke: Macmillan.

Audit Commission (2003) *Homelessness: Responding to the new agenda*, London: Audit Commission.

Balloch, S. and Jones, B. (1990) *Poverty and anti-poverty strategy: The local government response*, London: AMA.

Bevan, M., Kemp, P.A. and Rhodes, D. (1995) *Private landlords and Housing Benefit*, York: Centre for Housing Policy, University of York.

Biehal, N. and Wade, J. (1999) '"I thought it would be easier": the early housing careers of young people leaving care', in J. Rugg (ed) *Young people, housing and social policy*, London: Routledge, pp 79-92.

Biehal, N., Clayden, J. and Byford, S. (2000) *Preventative work with teenagers: Evaluation of an adolescent support team*, York: Joseph Rowntree Foundation Findings.

Borland, M. and Hill, M. (1996-97) 'Teenagers in Britain', *Youth and Policy*, no 55, pp 56-68.

Bramley, G. and Pawson, H. (2002) 'Low demand for housing: incidence, causes and UK national policy implications', *Urban Studies*, vol 39, no 3, pp 393-422.

Bryman, A. (1992) *Quantity and quality in social research*, London: Routledge.

Burchardt, T., Le Grand, J. and Piachaud, D. (2002) 'Degrees of exclusion: developing a dynamic, multi-dimensional measure', in J. Hills, J. Le Grand and D. Piachaud (eds) *Understanding social exclusion*, Oxford: Oxford University Press, pp 30-43.

Butler, K., Carlisle, B. and Lloyd, R. (1994) *Homelessness in the 1990s*, London: Shelter.

Byrne, T. (2000) *Local government in Britain*, London: Penguin Books.

Cairns, P. (2001) *Repeat homelessness in Scotland*, Research Precis No 138, Edinburgh: Scottish Homes.

Cameron, A. , Harrison, L., Burton, P. and Marsh, A. (2001) *Crossing the housing and care divide*, Findings, York: Joseph Rowntree Foundation.

Cameron, S. and Field, A. (2000) 'Community, ethnicity and neighbourhood', *Housing Studies*, vol 15, no 6, pp 827-43.

Campbell, B. (1984) *Wigan Pier revisited*, London: Virago Press Limited.

Campbell, B. (1993) *Goliath*, London: Methuen.

Chugg, A. (1998) *No entry*, Birmingham: National Rent Deposit Forum.

Cloke, P., Milbourne, P. and Widdowfield, R. (2000) 'Change but no change: dealing with homelessness under the 1996 Housing Act', *Housing Studies*, vol 15, no 6, pp 739-56.

Conway, J. (1988) *Prescription for poor health: The crisis for homeless families*, London: SHAC (the London Housing Advice Centre).

Craig, G. (1992) *Replacing the Social Fund: A strategy for change*, York: Joseph Rowntree Foundation.

Darke, J., Conway, J. and Holman, C. (1992) *Homes for our children*, London: National Housing Forum.

Dennis, N. and Erdos, G. (1993) *Families without fatherhood* (2nd edn), London: Institute of Economic Affairs Health and Welfare Unit.

DETR (Department of the Environment, Transport and the Regions) (1999a) *Housing Benefit and the private rented sector*, Housing Research Summary No 95, London: DETR.

DETR (1999b) *National strategy for neighbourhood renewal. Report of Policy Action Team 5 on Housing Management* at www.odpm.gov.uk/stellent/groups/ odpm_housing/documents/page/odpm_house_602432.hcsp

DETR (2001) *Supporting people: Policy into practice*, London: DETR.

DfES (Department for Education and Skills) (2001) *Lifelong Learning News*, Issue 2, summer (www.lifelonglearning.co.uk/iln/index.htm)

DfES (2003) *21st century skills: Realising our potential*, White Paper, London: Learning and Skills Development Agency.

DoE (Department of the Environment) (1994) *Access to local authority and housing association tenancies: A consultation paper*, London: DoE.

DoE (1997) *Financing temporary accommodation in the private rented sector: An economic analysis*, Housing Research Finding No 56, London: DoE.

DoH (Department of Health) (1999) *Me, survive out there?*, Green Paper, London: DoH.

DoH (2001) *New legislation to help young people leaving care*, Press Release 2001/0449, 27 September, at www.info.doh.gov.uk/doh/intpress.nsf/page/2001-0449?OpenDocument

DoH (2003a) *Continuing success of NHS services to help smokers quit*, Press Release 2003/0276, 24 July, at www.info.doh.gov.uk/doh/intpress.nsf/page/2003-0276?OpenDocument

DoH (2003b) *Statistics on smoking cessation service in England, April 2002 to March 2003*, Press Release 2003/0275, 24 July, at www.info.doh.gov.uk/doh/intpress.nsf/page/2003-0275?OpenDocument

Driver, S. and Martell, L. (2000) 'Left, Right and Third Way', *Policy & Politics*, vol 28, no 2, pp 147-61.

DSS (Department of Social Security) (1989) 'Extra help for 16 and 17 year olds', DSS Press Release 89/107, 13 March.

DTLR (Department for Transport, Local Government and the Regions) (2000) 'Government takes action to prevent youth homelessness', News Release 2000/0295, 11 April.

DTLR (2002a) *More than a roof: A report into tackling homelessness*, London: DTLR.

DTLR (2002b) *Homelessness strategies: A good practice handbook*, London: DTLR.

DTLR and Connexions (2001) *Working together: Connexions and youth homelessness agencies*, Nottingham: DfES publications.

DTLR and Teenage Pregnancy Unit (2001) *Guidelines for good practice in supported accommodation for young parents*, London: DTLR.

DWP (Department for Work and Pensions) (2003a) *Jobseeker's Allowance* at www.dwp.gov.uk/lifeevent/benefits/jobseeker's_allowance.asp#16

DWP (2003b) *16/17 year olds – Income Support* at www.dwp.gov.uk/gbi/5a64733.asp

Ellison, N. (1998) 'The changing politics of social policy', in N. Ellison and C. Pierson (eds) *Developments in British social policy*, Basingstoke: Macmillan, pp 31-45.

Ellison, N. and Pierson, C. (1998) 'Introduction', in N. Ellison and C. Pierson (eds) *Developments in British social policy*, Basingstoke: Macmillan, pp 1-14.

Evans, A. (1999) 'Rationing device or passport to social housing? The operation of the homelessness legislation in Britain in the 1990s', in S. Hutson and D. Clapham (eds) *Homelessness: Public policies and private troubles*, London: Cassell, pp 133-54.

Finn, D. (1984) 'Leaving school and growing up', in I. Bates, J. Clarke, P. Cohen, D. Finn, R. Moore and P. Willis (eds) *Schooling for the dole?*, Basingstoke: Macmillan, pp 17-64.

Fitzpatrick, S. (2000) *Young homeless people*, Basingstoke: Macmillan.

Fitzpatrick, S. and Klinker, S. (2000) *Research on single homelessness in Britain*, York: Joseph Rowntree Foundation Findings.

Fitzpatrick, S., Kemp, P. and Klinker, S. (2000) *Single homelessness: An overview of research in Britain*, Bristol/York: The Policy Press/Joseph Rowntree Foundation.

Forrest, R. and Murie, A. (1990) *Moving the housing market: Council estates, social change and privatization*, Aldershot: Avebury.

Foyer Federation (1998) *Foyers and the New Deal: Six months on*, London: Foyer Federation.

Franklin, B. (1998) 'Constructing a service: context and discourse in housing management', *Housing Studies*, vol 13, no 2, pp 201-16.

Franklin, B. and Clapham, D. (1997) 'The social construction of housing management', *Housing Studies*, vol 12, no 1, pp 7-26.

Furbey, R. A. (1999) 'Urban "regeneration": reflections on a metaphor', *Critical Social Policy*, vol 19, no 4, pp 419-45.

George, V. and Wilding, P. (1985) *Ideology and social welfare*, London: Routledge and Kegan Paul.

Gholam, G. (1993) *Before you go*, Leaving Home Project, London: Centrepoint.

Giddens, A. (2000) *The Third Way and its critics*, Cambridge: Polity Press.

Gilchrist, R. and Jeffs, T. (1995) 'Foyers: Housing solution or folly?', *Youth and Policy*, no 50, pp 1-12.

Gilroy, R. (1993) *Models of housing management in meeting the needs of young homeless people*, Departmental Working Paper 22, Department of Town and Country Planning, Newcastle upon Tyne: University of Newcastle upon Tyne.

Harding, J. (1997) *Preparing for experience: The effectiveness of leaving home and housing education*, Working Paper No 64, Newcastle upon Tyne: Department of Town and Country Planning, University of Newcastle upon Tyne.

Harding, J. (1999) 'Explanations of, and responses to, youth homelessness in local authority housing departments', *Local Government Studies*, vol 25, no 3, pp 58-69.

Harding, J. and Keenan, P. (1998) 'The provision of furnished accommodation by local authorities', *Housing Studies*, vol 13, no 3, pp 377-90.

Harding, J. and Kirk, R. (2002) 'Housing and support needs of teenage parents and pregnant teenagers', unpublished report to Newcastle City Council.

Harris, N. (1988) 'Social security and the transition to adulthood', *Journal of Social Policy*, vol 17, no 4, pp 502-23.

Harris, N. (1989) *Social security for young people*, Aldershot: Avebury.

Heron, E. and Dwyer, P. (1999) 'Doing the right thing: Labour's attempt to forge a new welfare deal between the individual and the welfare state', *Social Policy and Administration*, vol 33, no 1, pp 91-104.

Hills, J. (2002) 'Does a focus on "social exclusion" change the policy response?', in J. Hills, J. Le Grand and D. Piachaud (eds) *Understanding social exclusion*, Oxford: Oxford University Press, pp 226-43.

Home Office (2000) *Listen up*, London: Home Office.

Homelessness Directorate (2003) *Achieving positive outcomes on homelessness*, London: ODPM.

Housing Corporation, The (1996) *Housing associations and the Children Act*, Source 11, London: The Housing Corporation.

Housing Corporation, The (1997) *A housing plus approach to achieving sustainable communities*, London: The Housing Corporation.

Hudson, F. and Ineichen, B. (1991) *Taking it lying down*, Basingstoke: Macmillan.

Hutson, S. (1999) 'The experience of "homeless" accommodation and support', in S. Hutson and D. Clapham (eds) *Homelessness: Public policies and private troubles*, London: Cassell, pp 208-25.

Hutson, S. and Liddiard, M. (1991) *Young and homeless in Wales: Government policies, insecure accommodation and agency support*, Occasional Paper 26, Department of Sociology and Anthropology, Swansea: University College, Swansea.

Hutson, S. and Liddiard, M. (1994) *Youth homelessness*, Basingstoke: Macmillan.

Jones, C. and Murie, A. (1998) *Reviewing the right to buy*, York: Joseph Rowntree Foundation Findings.

Jones, C. and Novak, T. (1999) *Poverty, welfare and the disciplinary state*, London: Routledge.

Jones, G. (1995) *Leaving home*, Buckingham: Open University Press.

Kay, H. (1994) *Conflicting priorities*, London: CHAR and the Chartered Institute of Housing.

Keenan, P., Lowe, S. and Spencer, S. (1999) 'Housing abandonment in inner cities – the politics of low demand for housing', *Housing Studies*, vol 14, no 5, pp 703-16.

Killeen, D. (1988) *Estranged*, Edinburgh: Shelter Scottish Campaign for the Homeless.

Kirby, P. (1994) *A word from the street*, London: Centrepoint.

Kullberg, J. (2002) 'Consumers' responses to choice-based lettings mechanisms', *Housing Studies*, vol 17, no 4, pp 549-79.

Learning and Skills Council (2003) *The prospectus for the Entry to Employment Learning Framework*, Issue 04, 23 January, at www.lsc.gov.uk/NR/rdonlyres evvakzaqa4mbtpwfpxtpm5tnludy4siqgifkx5wjndfkdni64tkrs6yadyjyb7rygdlg 6wr34xqzpg/E2EProspectusIssue04.doc

Leather, P., Lee, P. and Murie, A. (2002) 'North East England: Changing housing markets and urban regeneration', Final Report, Executive Summary, Centre for Urban and Regional Studies, Birmingham: University of Birmingham.

Lee, P. and Murie, A. (1999) 'Spatial and social divisions within British cities: beyond residualisation', *Housing Studies*, vol 14, no 9, pp 625-40.

Lister, R. (2001) 'Doing good by stealth: the politics of poverty and inequality under New Labour', *New Economy*, vol 8, no 2, pp 65-70.

Lloyd, T. (1999) *Young men's attitude to gender and work*, York: Joseph Rowntree Foundation Findings.

Lund, B. (1996) *Housing problems and housing policy*, Harlow: Longman.

McCluskey, J. (1993) *Re-assessing priorities*, London: CHAR.

MacDonald, R. and Marsh, J. (2002) *Street corner society: Young people, social exclusion and leisure careers*, Brighton: ESRC Youth, Citizenship and Social Change Programme Conference, March.

Mack, J. and Lansley, S. (1985) *Poor Britain*, London: George Allen and Unwin.

MacLagan, I. (1993) *Four years' severe hardship*, Ilford: Youthaid and Barnardo's.

Malpass, P. and Murie, A. (1994) *Housing policy and practice*, Basingstoke: Macmillan.

Murray, C. (1990) 'Underclass', in R. Lister (ed) (1996) *Charles Murray and the underclass*, London: Institute of Economic Affairs Health and Welfare Unit, pp 23-53.

Murray, C. (1994) 'Underclass: The crisis deepens', in R. Lister (ed) (1996) *Charles Murray and the underclass*, London: Institute of Economic Affairs Health and Welfare Unit, pp 99-135.

National Children's Home (1993) *A lost generation?*, London: National Children's Home.

NCC (Newcastle City Council) (1982) 'Report to Homelessness Joint Sub-Committee', 28 October.

NCC (1983) 'Report to Homelessness Joint Sub-Committee', 27 October.

NCC (1984) 'Report to Homelessness Joint Sub-Committee', 26 April.

NCC (1985) 'Report to Special Needs Joint Sub-Committee', 24 October.

NCC (1988) 'Report to Special Needs Joint Sub-Committee', 27 October.

NCC (1989) 'Report to Policy and Resources Sub-Group', 3 August.

NCC (1990a) 'Report to Special Needs Joint Sub-Committee', 27 November.

NCC (1990b) 'Report to Housing Committee', 10 October.

NCC (1991a) *Housing Annual Report 1990/91*, Newcastle: NCC.

NCC (1991b) 'Report to Special Needs Joint Sub-Committee', 17 September.

NCC (1992) 'Report to Housing Committee', October.

NCC (1994a) *Survey of young people moving into independent living*, Newcastle: Chief Executive's Section, NCC.

NCC (1994b) 'Report to Housing Committee', 14 September.

NCC (1994c) 'Report to Housing/Social Services Liaison Sub-Committee', 21 June.

NCC (1996a) 'Report to Housing Committee', 19 November.

NCC (1996b) 'Report to Housing Committee', 10 April.

NCC (1996c) 'Report to Housing Committee', 11 December.

NCC (1997) 'Report to Housing and Social Services Sub-Committee', 17 June.

NCC (1998a) 'Report to Housing Committee', 9 December.

NCC (1998b) 'Report to Housing and Social Services Sub-Committee', 17 July.

NCC (2000) 'Going for growth East End and West End plans: The way forward', report by Chief Executive, 6 December.

NCC (2002) *Your choice homes: Homefinder lettings service*, Consultation Paper, November, Newcastle: Community and Housing Directorate, NCC.

NCC (2003a) *Attendance and absence in Newcastle schools*, at www.newcastle.gov.uk/educlibnew.nsf 32a7fbef52117a9b8025668e004f2c7b 51bee56bd146fa5480256b9800576121? OpenDocument&Highlight=2,attendance

NCC (2003b) *Newcastle upon Tyne secondary school performance: GCSE results 2002*, at www.newcastle.gov.uk/educlibnew.nsf/ a995f08678e0882f80256688005190dd/ d9a1ce559dcf2df380256cb40052291f?OpenDocument

NCC (2003c) *Newcastle schools summary* at www.newcastle.gov.uk/ educlibnew.nsf/a995f08678e0882f80256688005190dd/ 93b58bd96d920e9c80256b8800345689/$FILE/ Newcastle%20Summary%20GCSE%202002.pdf

NCC (2003d) *Newcastle street wardens*, at www.newcastle.gov.uk/nsw.nsf/a/ faqs?opendocument

NIN (Newcastle Independence Network) (1999) 'Annual Report 1998/99'.

ONS (Office for National Statistics) (2001) *Social trends 31*, London: The Stationery Office.

ONS (2003a) *Work based training for young people: By type of training, 1990-91 to 1998-99*, using Social Trends dataset, at www.statistics.gov.uk/statbase/ xsdataset.asp?vlnk=261&More=Y

ONS (2003b) *Statistics about Newcastle upon Tyne*, at http:// neighbourhood.statistics.gov.uk/ areaprofileframes.asp?aid=175547&hid=&tid=13&AREA =Newcastle%20upon%20Tyne

ONS (2003c) *Drug use among 16-29 year olds 2000: Regional trends 37*, at www.statistics.gov.uk/statbase/ssdataset.asp?vlnk=5938&More=Y

ODPM (Office of the Deputy Prime Minister) (2000) *Update Issue 21*, 14 June, at www.Office of the Deputy Prime Minister.gov.uk/stellent/groups/ Office of the Deputy Prime Minister_urbanpolicy/documents/page/Office of the Deputy Prime Minister_urbpol_608075.hcsp

ODPM (2001) *Preventing tomorrow's rough sleepers: A good practice handbook*, at www.odpm.gov.uk/stellent/groups/odpm_homelessness/documents/page/ odpm_home_601531.pdf

ODPM (2002) *Major boost for Merseyside regeneration*, News Release, 28 June, at www.odpm.gov.uk/pns/DisplayPN.cgi?pn_id=2002_0260

ODPM (2003a) *£1.5bn boost for better council housing*, News Release, 28 July, at www.odpm.gov.uk/pns/DisplayPN.cgi?pn_id=2003_0147

ODPM (2003b) *Choice-based lettings: Newsletter issue 5: winter 2003*, London: ODPM, at www.odpm.gov.uk/stellent/groups/odpm_housing/documents/pdf/odpm_house_pdf_609310.pdf

ODPM (2003c) *Market renewal pathfinders*, at www.odpm.gov.uk/stellent/groups/odpm_communities/documents/page/odpm_comm_023263.hcsp

ODPM (2003d) *Statement to the House of Commons on sustainable communities*, 5 February, at www.odpm.gov.uk/stellent/groups/odpm_about/documents/page/odpm_about_022611.hcsp

ODPM (2003e) *Preventing youth homelessness*, Housing Research Summary No 194, London: ODPM, at www.odpm.gov.uk/stellent/groups/odpm_housing/documents/page/odpm_house_609803.hcsp

Pawson, H. (1998) *Local authority stock turnover in the 1990s*, York: Joseph Rowntree Foundation Findings.

Petch, H., Cairns, B. and Wyler, S. (1994) *The bare necessities*, London: CHAR, London Homelessness Forum and Homeless Network.

Pierson, C. (1998) 'Theory in British social policy', in N. Ellison and C. Pierson (eds) *Developments in British social policy*, Basingstoke: Macmillan, pp 17-30.

Pleace, N. and Quilgars, D. (1999) 'Youth homelessness', in J. Rugg (ed) *Young people, housing and social policy*, London: Routledge, pp 93-108.

Pleace, N., Burrows, R. and Quilgars, D. (1997) 'Homelessness in contemporary Britain: Conceptualisation and measurement', in R. Burrows, N. Pleace and D. Quilgars (eds) *Homelessness and social policy*, London: Routledge, pp 1-18.

Pollhammer, M. and Grainger, P. (2003) *Housing on the horizon*, Housing and Community Research Group Discussion Paper No 1, Northumbria: Northumbria University.

Power, A. and Mumford, K. (1999) *The problem of low housing demand in inner cities*, York: Joseph Rowntree Foundation Findings.

QPID (Quality and Performance Improvement Dissemination) (2000) *TEC/CCTEs and the learning gateway*, Nottingham: DfEE publications, at www.dfes.gov.uk/studynet/exec87.pdf

Quilgars, D. and Anderson, I. (1995) *Foyers for young people*, York: Joseph Rowntree Housing Research Finding 142.

Quilgars, D. and Pleace, N. (1999) 'Housing and support services for young people', in J. Rugg (ed) *Young people, housing and social policy*, London: Routledge, pp 109-26.

Rahman, M., Palmer, G. and Kenway, P. (2001) *Monitoring poverty and social exclusion 2001*, York: Joseph Rowntree Foundation Findings.

Randall, G. and Brown, S. (1994) *The move in experience*, London: Crisis.

Ratcliffe, P. (1998) '"Race", housing and social exclusion', *Housing Studies*, vol 13, no 6, pp 807-18.

Reid, P. and Klee, H. (1999) 'Young homeless people and service provision', *Health and Social Care in the Community*, vol 7, no 1, pp 17-24.

Richards, J. (1992) 'A sense of duty', in C. Grant (ed) *Built to last*, *Roof* Magazine, pp 129-38.

Roaf, C. and Lloyd, C. (1995) *Multi-agency work with young people in difficulty*, York: Joseph Rowntree Foundation Social Care Research Findings 68.

Rooney, B. (1997) *The viability of furnished tenancies in social housing*, York: Joseph Rowntree Housing Research Findings 224.

Rough Sleepers Unit (2001) *Coming in from the cold: Second progress report on the government's strategy on rough sleeping – summer 2001*, London: Rough Sleepers Unit.

Ryan, M. (1999) *The Children Act 1989: Putting it into practice*, Aldershot: Ashgate.

Scottish Executive (2002) *Report from the Working Group on the Throughcare and Aftercare of Looked After Children in Scotland*, Edinburgh: Scottish Executive at www.scotland.gov.uk/library5/education/tcac.pdf

Scottish Executive (2003) *Parliament passes homelessness bill*, Edinburgh: Scottish Executive News Release SESJ202/2003, 5 March.

SEU (Social Exclusion Unit) (1998) *Truancy and school exclusion*, London: The Stationery Office.

SEU (1999a) *Teenage pregnancy*, London: The Stationery Office.

SEU (1999b) *Bridging the gap: New opportunities for 16-18 year olds not in education, employment or training*, London: The Stationery Office.

SEU (2000a) *Young people*, Policy Action Team Report 12, London: The Stationery Office.

SEU (2000b) *National strategy for neighbourhood renewal report of Policy Action Team 4: Neighbourhood management*, London: ODPM.

SEU (2001a) *Preventing social exclusion*, London: SEU.

SEU (2001b) *A new commitment to neighbourhood renewal: National strategy action plan*, London: SEU.

SEU (2002) *Reducing re-offending by ex-prisoners*, London: SEU.

Shaw, K., Todorovic, J. and Gill, E. (1996) *Preparing for competition: The introduction of CCT for housing management*, University of Northumbria at Newcastle: Public Policy Research Unit.

Smith, J., Gilford, S. and O'Sullivan, A. (1998) *The family background of young homeless people*, London: Family Policy Studies Centre.

Somerville, P. (1999) 'The making and unmaking of homelessness legislation', in S. Hutson and D. Clapham (eds) *Homelessness: Public policies and private troubles*, London: Cassell, pp 29-57.

Speak, S. (1995) *The difficulties of setting up home for young single mothers*, York: Joseph Rowntree Social Policy Research Findings 72.

Steele, A. (2002) 'Black youth homelessness', in P. Somerville and A. Steele (eds) *'Race', housing and social exclusion*, London: Jessica Kingsley, pp 178-91.

Stewart, G. and Stewart, J. (1991) *Relieving poverty*, London: AMA.

Stoker, G. (1991) *The politics of local government*, Basingstoke: Macmillan.

Strathdee, R. (1993) *Housing our children*, London: Centrepoint.

Third, H., Pawson, H. and Tate, J. (2001) *Sustaining young people's tenancies in the social rented sector: The South Clyde experience*, School of Planning and Housing, Edinburgh: Edinburgh College of Art/Heriot-Watt University.

Venn, S. (1985) *Singled out*, London: CHAR.

Walker, R. M. (2000) 'The changing management of social housing: the impact of externalism and managerialism, *Housing Studies*, vol 15, no 2, pp 281-99.

Watchman, P. Q. and Robson, P. (1989) *Homelessness and the law in Britain*, Glasgow: The Planning Exchange.

Young, K. and Davies, M. (1990) *The politics of local government since Widdicombe*, York: Joseph Rowntree Foundation.

Index

Page references for figures and tables are in *italics*; those for notes are followed by n

U

V

W

Y

Also available from The Policy Press

Housing associations – rehousing women leaving domestic violence
New challenges and good practice
Cathy Davis
Paperback £19.99 (US$32.00) ISBN 1 86134 489 9
234 x156mm 192 pages July 2003

Managing public services innovation
The experience of English housing associations
Richard M. Walker, Emma L. Jeanes and Robert O. Rowlands
Paperback £18.99 (US$31.00) ISBN 1 86134 294 2
234 x156mm 144 pages April 2001

Two steps forward
Housing policy into the new millennium
Edited by David Cowan and Alex Marsh
Paperback £19.99 (US$32.50) ISBN 1 86134 229 2
Hardback £50.00 (US$69.95) ISBN 1 86134 252 7
216 x148mm 408 pages July 2001

Housing, social policy and difference
Disability, ethnicity, gender and housing
Malcolm Harrison and Cathy Davis
Paperback £19.99 (US$32.50) ISBN 1 86134 187 3
Hardback £50.00 (US$75.00) ISBN 1 86134 305 1
216 x148mm 256 pages April 2001

Home ownership in a risk society
A social analysis of mortgage arrears and possessions
Janet Ford, Roger Burrows and Sarah Nettleton
Paperback £19.99 (US$32.50) ISBN 1 86134 261 6
Hardback £50.00 (US$75.00) ISBN 1 86134 262 4
216 x148mm 212 pages July 2001

Inclusive housing in an ageing society
Innovative approaches
Edited by Sheila M. Peace and Caroline Holland
Paperback £19.99 (US$32.50) ISBN 1 86134 263 2
Hardback £50.00 (US$69.95) ISBN 1 86134 345 0
216 x148mm 280 pages October 2001

The private rented sector in a new century
Revival or false dawn?
Edited by Stuart Lowe and David Hughes
Paperback £21.99 (US$32.50) ISBN 1 86134 348 5
Hardback £50.00 (US$69.95) ISBN 1 86134 349 3
234 x156mm 240 pages September 2002

Maturing assets
The evolution of stock transfer housing associations
Hal Pawson and Cathie Fancy
Paperback £14.95 (US$25.50) ISBN 1 86134 545 3
A4 REPORT 72 pages September 2003
Published in association with the Joseph Rowntree Foundation

Social market or safety net?
British social rented housing in a European context
Mark Stephens, Nicky Burns and Lisa MacKay
Paperback £12.95 (US$23.50) ISBN 1 86134 387 6
A4 REPORT 64 pages February 2002
Published in association with the Joseph Rowntree Foundation

Changing places
Housing association policy and practice on nominations
and lettings
Hal Pawson and David Mullins
Paperback £19.99 (US$31.95) ISBN 1 86134 507 0
A4 REPORT 152 pages March 2003

Remote control
Housing associations and e-governance
Martyn Pearl and Martina Scanlon
Paperback £15.99 (US$26.95) ISBN 1 86134 398 1
A4 REPORT 72 pages February 2002

To order further copies of this publication or any other Policy Press title please contact:

In the UK and Europe:
Marston Book Services, PO Box 269,
Abingdon, Oxon, OX14 4YN, UK
Tel: +44 (0)1235 465500,
Fax: +44 (0)1235 465556,
Email: direct.orders@marston.co.uk

In the USA and Canada:
ISBS, 920 NE 58th Street, Suite 300,
Portland, OR 97213-3786, USA
Tel: +1 800 944 6190 (toll free),
Fax: +1 503 280 8832,
Email: info@isbs.com

In Australia and New Zealand:
DA Information Services, 648
Whitehorse Road, Mitcham,
Victoria 3132, Australia
Tel: +61 (3) 9210 7777,
Fax: +61 (3) 9210 7788,
E-mail: service@dadirect.com.au

Further information about all of our
titles can be also be found on our
website:

www.policypress.org.uk